I0484226

Leading the Big Show
Evolving Beyond Retail Management

To my family, for their constant love and support.
And for my husband, Dean, who seems to magically know exactly
what I need, at precisely the right moment.

Table of Contents

Introduction

I believe that as a retail leader you hold a wealth of power in your hands. You have the unique ability to impact the world on a number of levels. You have the power to build your company's business. You and your team are the face of your company. You are the ones your customers interact with everyday, and it's those interactions that support or destroy your company's brand. Your ability to successfully guide your team impacts and strengthens the company. The stronger you are, the stronger your company.

You have the power to positively affect each and every customer who walks through your doors. You can make their lives better with your products. You can impact their perception of themselves with your words and treatment of them. You have the power to enhance their day by the way you run your store and how you coach your team. It's in the exceptional experience you create for your customers that keep them coming back to see you, along with recommending you to their friends. There is no better compliment - or marketing - than that kind of recommendation.

Finally, I believe the greatest of all your powers as a retail leader lies in your ability to coach and mentor your team. You have the power to cultivate success in every single person you hire and guide. When you help them achieve their goals you help them build their self-confidence. That self-confidence will shape the person they are to become in the future and give them the ability to positively affect their world around them.

When you truly step into your power, you set the stage to create something more than just a "retail store." Like the centre ring in a circus, you can create an experience like no other.

You can create *The Big Show*.

Reaching the level of the Big Show moves you beyond just managing your store, to evolving into a true leader who has exactly what it take to make a big impact, and drive big results!

This book will help you think differently, make you more efficient and self-confident, and realize you have the gift to inspire *anyone* who walks through your doors.

You are a Leader. Show them the way.

Who Are You?

Understanding who you are guides you towards the leader you're meant to be.

Your True Worth

Leadership: The art of getting someone else to do something you want done because he wants to do it. ~ Dwight D. Eisenhower

As the Leader of the Big Show, it's difficult to give yourself a value because you are truly worth much more than just your hourly wage. A business coach and friend of mine, wrote a great blog about how a business owner can calculate their monetary worth per hour based on their responsibilities. I feel this calculation translates well for any retail leader.

The basis of his theory is that most people would probably say their net worth in dollars per hour equates to the hourly wage they receive, but that is not really true. As the leader of your business, you are actually responsible for the gross sales of the store for the entire year. That's right, the entire twelve months! Break down that dollar amount into an hourly wage, and it's much more than what you make an hour. Are your eyes being opened as you realize that your time is actually an extremely valuable commodity?

Let's break this down: If your business takes in 3 million dollars in a year, your hourly wage, based on a 40-hour work week for the year, means you are actually worth a little over $1440 per hour. I'm going to guess that this is significantly more than your hourly wage.
Now, here's the kicker. You now have to evaluate the tasks you take on during the day based on that hourly worth. Naturally, there are some things you have to do as a retail leader, but there are also many tasks you do in the run of a day that you could easily hand off to someone else. Let's use scheduling as an example. Ultimately, you as the leader of your business, are and should be held responsible for the wages you spend in your store. However, that doesn't mean you need to spend an hour or more a week creating a schedule and making the inevitable changes to it after it's posted. If you handed that task off to a trusted supervisor, it might take you 5 minutes to review the schedule, and then you could use the other 55 minutes to do sales coaching with your staff members. Since direct coaching can increase the sales performance of your staff, it will have a greater impact on your overall sales than it would have if you

continued to take the time to complete the schedule. Increasing your store's sales, in turn, will make a further increase in your hourly worth to the company.

From here on in ask yourself, "Is this task actually worth the hours I am putting into it, or could I be more effective elsewhere?"

It's All Perception

Never mistake activity for achievement. ~ John Wooden

I was having difficulty comprehending a co-worker's flustered drama over a project we were working on that had, in my opinion, an easily attainable deadline. I went to my manager for guidance.

She said, "Some people are busy, and some people are just busy in their heads."

Which are you?

The Flawed Character

Think about your favourite characters from books you've read, or from movies and television shows. The ones most people connect with are usually the ones that are flawed in some way. It's those flaws that make the character human and relatable. Flaws allow you to sympathize or empathize, and put yourself in their shoes. They aren't perfect at all. In fact, those characters that are perfect, or at least, think that they're perfect, are probably the characters you love to hate.

As a leader, you have to be like those characters you love, and be willing to show your flaws. You have to be willing to show you make mistakes, just like everyone else on your team, and that you too are vulnerable. A great leader will admit their mistakes when they happen and learn from them. By showing those realities, it shows you aren't perfect. People are better able to relate to you because you really aren't so different from them. When you can show that you've walked the same path they're walking now, and that you've learned a lot of lessons along the way, they'll be more willing to trust that you know what you're talking about.

Share your stories and your mistakes, but most of all, share your lessons. These are the things that great leaders are made of.

Branding

As a retail leader, it's important to have a good understanding of branding, what your company's brand actually is, and how you can uphold that brand in your store. It's also important to recognize that you have your own personal brand that needs to be developed as a retail leader. The stronger your brand, the better the connection will be to those who follow you.

I love how Roy H. Williams, aka the Wizard of Ads, explains branding in his book, *Secret Formulas of the Wizard of Ads: Turning Paupers into Princes and Lead into Gold.* He likens branding to Pavlov's dog. For those who don't know the story, Nobel Prize winner Ivan Pavlov created a salivation response in a dog by ringing a bell before giving the dog a meat paste. After much repetition, the dog started to salivate when it heard the bell ring, in anticipation of tasting meat. He created a physical reaction to the abstract association that the sound of the bell meant food.

That's exactly what you need to do with branding. Create an association that makes people "salivate" or think of your business, your product, or of you, in a way they can relate into their lives.

To me, one of the greatest branding campaigns ever implemented was the one of diamonds being a symbol of love. Brilliant (Pun intended)! Seriously though, there is nothing about this piece of carbon that makes it a symbol of what we feel. Yes, it's sparkly and pretty when it's cut just right, but in its true physical essence, it's cold and inanimate. Definitely not how most of us would describe our feelings for someone we love. Yet, we equate the diamond with those emotions because over and over again, it's been marketed to us that the diamond is a symbol of everlasting love. And the bigger the diamond the better. That's branding. That's exactly what you need to create the Big Show right in your store.

Thinking of companies like Harley Davidson, Starbucks, Apple and Coca Cola, you will definitely have clear ideas of what they stand for, good or bad, in your own opinion. While Coke has had different tag lines over the years, the one thing they have been consistent about in all their marketing messages and branding, is drinking Coke makes the world a better place. From their message of "I'd like to buy the world a Coke and keep it company," to the polar bears they are working towards saving today, they are consistent with that message.

Now, in terms of personal brands, think of Gandhi, Hitler, Martin Luther King Jr., and Martha Stewart. Each one of them brings an associative thought about what they stand for, or stood for. It's very clear. Their personal actions in every way support what they have projected as their personal brand. Contemplating a picture of Hitler snuggling puppies doesn't work in our heads, because his brand wasn't about warmth, love and happiness; but a picture of Martha Stewart in a lumberjack outfit wielding a chain saw might work, if she was showing us how to make our own rustic picnic bench.

On a personal level, the people around us also have associated thoughts about our qualities. Nice, creative, rebellious, helpful, resourceful and so forth, are all descriptions that could be correlated to our own selves and our attributes. We project our brand everyday through our actions and words. As the Leader of the Big Show, you must craft the brand that people want to follow. The key is to consistently drive how you want people to think of you, through those things. Every day you work towards this.

Whether it's personal, product, or company branding, you have to figure out what you or it stands for, and what that projection will be to the world. On a more philosophical level, it's really the purpose for being here. Everything after that needs to come back to that purpose. If you are wishy-washy on it, or send different messages with different purposes, people won't understand it because it's not clear in its intent or messaging.

For a product or a business, all the marketing you do has to centre on the purpose. The more you stay on target with it, the more people will understand it, and the stronger the brand will be. When you have that, the more likely it will be for people to associate with it and want to incorporate it into their lives. That's why it's so important for you to understand your company's brand, as a retail leader, so you can keep that in the forefront of your customer's minds every day.

On a personal level, your brand will be reflected in the company you work for, the actions you take during the day, and the way you talk to and build the people around you. When all of those align, everyone will have a clear sense of who you are, why you're here, and how you will impact the world around you.

Bottom line in branding: be consistent in everything you do *because* it sends a message.

Are You Biting the Bullet?

There are some leaders inspire people so greatly that their followers would gladly take a bullet for them.

There are other leaders who's people would more happily use them as a shield.

Do you know which you are? Why?

Becoming an Elite Athlete

Become your most true self day in and day out to best serve your team and your higher purpose.

The Elite Athlete

Before you can win, you have to believe you are worthy. ~ Mike Ditka

To become the best in the world, you have to operate under different ideals, and develop skills that the average person doesn't have. Looking at the upper echelon of athletes, no matter what the sport, they all have a set of characteristics that help to make them successful.

Elite athletes have chosen their sport and developed their position within the sport. They've figured out exactly where their skills work best. Whether it's a sprinter, a linebacker, pitcher, or swimmer they all have their specialties. They've focused and honed their skill set to be the best in their particular area.

The determination of the elite athlete is an amazing thing. Hours and hours of training, practice, and competition go into developing their skill at their chosen sport. Their mindset is to be the best, and that requires them to do whatever they have to, to be at the top of their game. Getting up early, squeezing in workouts, battling mental fatigue, and physical stress, are all part of that game. Heart and soul, they are committed. What defines the difference between the elite and the average is the mindset to never quit, and, above all, the supreme belief that they will win.

The best athletes in the world have great coaches. They don't ask their best friend for advice, they get someone who knows the game to teach and develop their training, so they can improve their skills and become better at what they do. Looking at elite mixed martial artists, they have different coaches for their specialized martial art, boxing, kickboxing, wrestling, strength training, conditioning, and even meditation. Every part of their game is continually broken down and refined. They learn from the best coaches in every area to sharpen their skills. When they've learned what they can, they move to another coach to keep their development moving forward. To be the best, means you have to always be looking to get better in each area of the profession. It's the continual coaching and learning that leads to even greater success.

World-class athletes continually set new goals for themselves. They always look to better their last performance. For the swimmer or sprinter, 1/100th of a second can be the difference between receiving a medal on the podium, or watching the medal presentations from the sidelines. Continually striving to be better makes all the difference in the world.

Elite athletes know that nutrition is key to keeping the body performing at its peak level. They often have strict diets when training, so they can make the most of their performance. Better nutrition means the body is fuelled properly, so it can work efficiently. The body functions properly, the brain has mental clarity, and together, that helps to create the best athlete possible.

As an elite retail leader, you are really no different than that world-class athlete. To be the best, you have to do all the things that will make you so. Know your talents and how you can best suit your team. Have the attitude that you will win, and that practice simply hones the best of your skills. Get a coach to keep improving. Continually set goals, so you can reach for that ring. And treat your body and your mind well; they are your best assets.

The Vision and the Mission

In Simon Sinek's book, Start *with WHY*, he discusses the difference between a vision statement and a mission statement. A **vision statement** is your purpose. Your reason for being here. Why you are doing what you are doing. Your **mission statement** is how you are going to accomplish your vision statement. It's the things you will do to make it happen.

Looking at them separately, you can see there is a real difference. The vision statement is intangible. It's an idea, a purpose, a direction. It doesn't have a physical embodiment to it. Whereas, the mission statement defines the physical ways of accomplishing the intangible idea proposed in the vision statement. It's the plan or the way you will go about achieving it.

Let's break it down.

My personal vision statement is: "I'm here to inspire and positively affect the people and businesses in my life, and the new ones I meet each day." This is my personal reason for being here, and how I plan to change the world around me.

My mission statement is: "I will make my vision happen by giving a sincere compliment, writing, blogging, speaking, coaching, mentoring and sharing my ideas. I will make the people and businesses in my life stronger by networking them together, so they can have an impact on each other, and the world around them." These are the physical steps I will take to make sure my vision happens.

The moment I put this together, I gained real clarity, not just in my business, but also in my life. I understood what I needed to do, where I needed to go, and how I was going to accomplish it.

When you want to be a remarkable leader, your purpose has to be far greater than just assisting customers to make purchases that have a positive impact on their lives. If that were the case, you would probably have maintained a sales position within your company, since you would be able to more directly affect the customer on a one-to-one basis. You would never have the inspiration to be more than that, because you would have been satisfied since you would be fulfilling your purpose.

Moving into a leadership position means you want to affect the company you work for in a greater way, and you want to have an impact on the people around you. There is a specific reason why you have those aspirations. Your reason will be uniquely yours, and you need to explore it for yourself to gain your own clarity.

Once you figure out your purpose, or your "why," it will be easy to figure out how you are going to accomplish it; by doing so, you will find you have greater appreciation for yourself and your reason for being here. Won't that be satisfying?

One More Guest

One of the greatest blessings I've had in my career is to be surrounded by passionate people, from the team around me, to my superiors who guided me along the way. I've had many opportunities to develop myself through them, both personally and professionally.

One completely eye-opening experience for me came from the owner of the retail chain I worked for. I remember him coming into the office, just vibrating with excitement about the speech he was going to deliver at our manager's meeting the following day, and then the following week for his industry peers at an international trade show. Now, the owner was always (and still is) passionate about his business, and that comes through when he talks about it. But, when he's truly excited about something, he's much like a child on Christmas Eve. This excitement was contagious, so I was very much looking forward to what he had to say.

At the meeting, when he got up to speak, the energy bouncing off of him was palpable.

"One more guest," he said and stopped. The grin spread across his face. He looked at us with anticipation.

If you're like me, I was thinking "Really? What the heck is this?" The faces around me pretty much reflected what was going through my head.

And then he started the presentation.

It all centred on helping one more guest in the store each hour. A guest who was *already* there to buy. That was it.

No extra marketing. No need to change your style. No extra work added to the workday. No more people onto your floor.

Simply just get your staff to help one person who was serving himself or herself, instead of letting them go to the cash register on their own.

The numbers he generated based on the averages in the stores were staggering.

Here's what he did, and how you can do it yourself.

Analyze each sale that goes through your cash register. You should notice that each time a customer is helped by one of your sales team, the average sale is higher than those who self help. If it's not, you have a much bigger issue to fix first: Why have a sales team if they don't increase your sales?

The difference between the assisted and unassisted sale will vary from business to business depending on the service provided. For example, electronics are generally much more expensive than clothes on the overall, so the electronics store should have much higher sales numbers than the clothing store, based on the average sale.

For our purposes, we'll use round numbers so we can calculate easily.

Let's say the average sale is $50.00 when a customer is helped by a sales associate but only $40.00 when the customer shops on his or her own. So, we make $10.00 more on every sale that is assisted by a sales person.

Now, let's say our store is open 10 hours a day, every day. Helping one more customer an hour, over the 10 hours you are open, will increase the sales by $100.00 a day.

This would add about $3,000.00 a month to your sales.

That equals $36,000 a year.

$36K! That's an awesome increase by simply focusing on the people who are *already* there in your store and ready to buy something from you.

The question he asked us, and now I am asking you is, can you and your team collectively help one more person each hour than you are helping right now?

You know you can.

Boost Your Brain Power

Drink water regularly throughout the day. It will give you more energy and better mental clarity. Your brain needs to be hydrated in order to function properly.

Your brain also uses glucose to create the energy it needs to make decisions. When you want to be at the top of your game, feed your body so you can boost your brainpower.

Sharpening the Knives

To do great things is difficult; but to command great things is more difficult. ~ Friedrich Nietzsche

At one point or another, we've all heard or used the term he's "not the sharpest knife in the drawer." For some, it might be a true statement, but for most it's probably because the knife has never been properly introduced to the sharpening stone. Training is the sharpening stone in the corporate world. The success of an employee is often dependent on the type of training he or she gets. The better the training, the sharper the knife, as it were.

A few simple steps can get your training on the right track to produce successful employees right out of the gate.

1. Consider the training materials. Even if you don't have a complete guide for the position, a reference guide or a cheat sheet is fairly easy to create. It will give the employee the ability to refer back to it regularly, cutting down the number of questions (or repeat questions) they might have down the road. Reference guides are perfect for those processes that are lengthier and take longer to absorb, like using a particular computer program to complete paperwork. Even something as simple as answering the phone with the right greeting can be written down, so there's no room for error. These reference sheets also make more independent employees, allowing you to focus on the business.

   Remember, any task that's key to the job should have a reference sheet.

2. Each person has a specific primary learning style. They will fall into one of three categories: visual, auditory or kinaesthetic. Visual learners need to see how it's done. Auditory learners need to listen to the trainer as they walk through the material. Kinaesthetic learners need to learn through touch and movement. Include all the learning styles in

your training to make it really successful. Not only will you connect with all the learning styles, it will make the training more interesting because you won't be doing the same thing all the time. Ensure there are visual references like drawings on a white board, a training guide, or a computer screen. Cover the material verbally, even if it's just quick review points. And be sure to have training elements that physically engage the employee. Physically doing the task or completing a review test are a couple of ways to incorporate the kinaesthetic element.

3. Finally, make sure the person can show you how to do each task trained. It's the only way to make sure they clearly understand what they have to do.

    First, show them how the task is done. Next, coach them through the task as they do it. Finally, ask the person to show you how to do it on his or her own.

    The repetition helps to solidify the material and if they can complete the task with no coaching, then you know they have it, and there will be no room for excuses in the future for not completing it properly.

Creating a great training program in your store will produce people that are much more efficient, confident and happy in their positions.

Be the Best

From the front, middle, or back of the pack, it's the actions that define the leader, not the position.

What actions are you taking to be the best leader you can each day?

Creative Scheduling

Controlling your wages has an immediate and direct effect on your bottom line profits. It's one of the largest things as a retail leader that you can directly control. Rethinking how you schedule the hours you have available each day can make a big difference.

Try this:

Think of your busiest day of the week. Instead of scheduling one 8-hour shift in the middle of that day when your traffic is at its peak, try using two 4-hours shifts during the busiest period. It's the same number of hours used, but much more effective on your sales floor. Extra people on your sales floor will increase your sales during your busiest times because you'll have more staff on hand to assist your customers. As an added bonus, it will make your life less hectic, and it should make your customers more satisfied with your service, since they can get the help they need when they want it. Best of all, you can accomplish it without adding extra hours to your schedule.

Now let's get really crazy….

Three people scheduled into 3-hour shifts, instead of one 8-hour shift. Insane, right?! But think of battling that crazy rush hour with two extra people. Won't that be so much better? But, you say, that's nine hours not eight, and that means I have one extra hour added into my schedule. Easy. Make one of the eight-hour shifts in your schedule for the week a 7-hour shift and you're golden. Or, cut two shifts by 30 minutes each. When you think it through and play with some numbers, you will see that you can easily do this.

The biggest hurdle retail leaders have to get over with this kind of scheduling is basing the schedule on the needs of the store rather than the needs of the people on your team. There always has to be a balance, but realistically, in retail, there are always people who are happy to work the shorter shifts.

Break Schedule

Timing is everything in the centre ring of the Big Show. It's the same for you store. You need to control the timing. Every morning, as part of your opening duties, you should create a break schedule for the staff working that day. First and foremost, creating a break schedule is courteous to your staff. When you have a break schedule in place, every person on your team knows when it's their turn to relax, and can make plans accordingly. It also stops arguments before they happen, about whose turn it is to go for a break.

Creating a break schedule is also a part of good sales management. When done properly, you'll schedule your breaks around your busiest periods of the day. If you have a rush between 12pm and 1pm, then you will avoid scheduling breaks during that time, in order to increase customer service during those rushes.

A break schedule also helps to ensure you don't have two people gone on a break from the same department at the same time. You want to ensure you have the most coverage on your sales floor at all times. When it's necessary to have overlapping breaks, it's best to make sure they come from different areas, so you're not completely depleting one department of its staff members.

Your break schedule can also include the person who will cover the section while the other person is on their break. For instance, if you have a cashier gone for their lunch break, you may need a supervisor to cover the cash area while they're gone. Having it listed on the schedule makes everyone aware of his or her responsibilities.

Since everyone checks the break schedule, it's also a great place to assign the store's cleaning sections during the day, list any extra tasks you need your team members to do, and you can also assign necessary opening and closing duties.

A sample schedule might look like this:

Name	Break Time	Coverage	Section Assignment	Extra Tasks
Joe (cashier)	11:30am-12:00pm	Anne	Opening cashier duties	Reorganize cash shelves
Anne (sales dept. 1 and cashier)	1:30pm-2:00pm	Melissa	Close Rows 1-8	Tidy displays in Rows 1-8
Melissa (sales dept 2)	2:00pm-2:30pm	Simon	Close Rows 9-16	Clean bathroom

A break schedule also makes your life easier, because you will have less people asking you questions about their responsibilities and timing of their breaks. Fewer disruptions will make you more efficient.

Time After Time

It's not the hours you put in; it's what you put in the hours. ~ Unknown

Be efficient. Be effective. Get it done.

The Cost of Turnover

It's a very good exercise to determine the actual cost of turnover for your company and quite surprising how much money you actually spend.

Some of the hard costs are easy to determine, like the cost of advertising for the position, the hourly wage of the person reviewing the interview and the ones conducting the interviews. There is also the cost to set the new person up on payroll, benefits and their computer. Plus the hard costs of training materials, and of course the in person training itself. Not only do you have to include the cost of the employee but also the cost of the trainer. You should also include the costs of training for the person that just left the company since it is a complete loss.

Let's break it down to see what it might look like for an average store. We will use an average wage of $15 per hour for the employees, and $20 per hour for trainers and supervisors.

Two hours write, place and follow up on the ad by a supervisor = $40
Advertising for ad (cost can be anywhere from $100– $3000) = $1000
Two hours to review and shortlist resumes by a supervisor = $40
Interview #1 for 6 candidates with review time by a supervisor (7 hours) = $140
Interview #2 for 4 candidates with review time by a supervisor (6 hours) = $120
Interview #3 for 2 candidates with review time by a supervisor (3 hours) = $60
Hiring paperwork 1 hour = $20
Payroll, benefits and computer set up (1 hour) = $20
Basic Orientation and Training (6 hours) employee = $90
Basic Orientation and Training (6 hours) trainer = $120
Departmental Training (20 hours) employee = $300
Departmental Training (20 hours) trainer = $400
Training materials = $100

Total cost = $2450.00

And this is without calculating costs that are much harder to determine, like the loss of customers that the employee might take with them. Knowledge of your business and products. Loss of sales directly because the new person will not be up to speed. And there is the loss of productivity for the position that is being replaced, for the person taking time to learn and for the supervisors and/or peers that are assisting to coach the new employee.

On top of all that, based on a 5% bottom line, you would have to generate $49 000.00 just to break even for the new hire based only on the total cost of $2450.00.

When you take a look at the numbers, it makes a lot of sense to create an environment where the employees want to stay, learn and work.

More Than You Need

We've all been stuck behind the eight ball when we've had somebody call in sick or quit, and had nobody on our staff list we could call in to help. The key to keeping your sanity is to have more staff then you need for your schedule.

Now, many retail leaders say to me, "If I have too many staff members I won't be able to give them the hours they want."

To that, I say, so what?

You're a business, not a day-care. Certainly, if you want to create the Big Show experience, you have to be more than just average, and that is directly evident in your sales. Brilliant retail stores do brilliant sales numbers. If your staff members want to get more hours, they need to work for it. There is absolutely nothing wrong with that. In fact, it makes perfect sense, because it is a give and take of equality. They work hard and you will give them hours. Why do you want a person on the floor who doesn't do their job the way they're supposed to do it? That's simply rewarding poor behaviour, when you could be rewarding great behaviour.

Having more staff than you need puts you in a fantastic position. First of all, you'll no longer have to struggle to cover shifts when someone is sick or on vacation. And if someone quits or if you have to fire someone, you have a back-up team. Imagine how great that will be!

Next, it'll also allow you to schedule people based on their performance, meaning your best staff members get the best shifts. Period. Then everyone else gets what's left over. That means you'll have your best people working at the best times you can have them work. And eventually those duds that you have on your staff will work their way out the door.

Finally, it will give you more passionate people working more often. Your staff morale will increase, since everyone will be working hard toward the same goal, and not just coasting. You'll have less stress and more efficiency. That means you will increase the customer service in your store, customer satisfaction will start to skyrocket and, if that wasn't enough, you'll increase sales.

Start hiring. And keep doing it. There's a gem or two out there, just waiting for you to find them.

The Dead Horses

A general is just as good or just as bad as the troops under his command make him. ~ General Douglas MacArthur

I was once at a conference where a speaker was metaphorically talking about the dead horses on a retail sales team. Those individuals who just can't seem to do their jobs no matter what you do to try to get them to do it. Inevitably, as retail leaders, we think there is something more we can do to inspire our dead horses.

I was so happy to find a list on **mazepath.com**, of the crazy things we might try to get the dead horses to work better for us. While there were many, I picked a few that amused me the most.

1. Change the riders. Another rider might handle the horse better.
2. Buy a stronger whip and beat the dead horse.
3. Attend a dead horse motivational seminar.
4. Point the dead horse in the opposite direction and note how well he maintains his position.
5. Reclassify the dead horse as living impaired.
6. Do a time management study to see if lighter riders would improve productivity.
7. Upgrade the dead horse's working conditions.
8. Shorten the track.
9. Create a training seminar to increase the rider's load share.
10. Harness several dead horses together for increased speed.

The bottom line is the dead horses are a waste of valuable time. You can't motivate or inspire a dead horse. Just lay them to rest.

Just to the Bar

Look for people who will aim for the remarkable, who will not settle for the routine. ~ David Ogilvy

A very successful businessman said to me, "It's so easy to fire the people on your staff that aren't working out. The hardest ones to fire are the ones that only work to bar. They do their job, but nothing more. They're the ones that are holding your company back."

When he said it, a light went on for me, and I realized he was completely right.

When you have an environment at work where you encourage growth, idea sharing, and the drive to simply be better, the person who isn't going above and beyond isn't adding to that culture. They *are* holding the business back.

Yes, they are steady. And yes, they get their work done. But that's it.

I firmly believe in this quote from Harry J. Friedman, an internationally acclaimed retail consultant, **"As a business or store, you're either getting better or getting worse."**

When you have someone that just doesn't see the business the same way you do, and they are only in it for the pay-cheque, they just aren't going to make the decisions you need them to make in order to advance your company. This is not someone who can or will create the experience you need to create for the Big Show.

What if you replaced that person with one who saw the business the way you do? Who had passion for it and a similar drive to the rest of the team? What could you accomplish then? Would you be able to exceed your targets more regularly? Would you be more successful? The answer is yes, you would.

If you want your business to grow, you *must* exceed your targets. You have to continually evolve. You have to have staff members

---

that inspire creativity and are always thinking of ways to make things better, for the business and for each other. That is what will make your business stronger and better, and give it the razzle-dazzle it needs to take its spot in the centre ring.

Take a Real Break

Leave your store on your break and shut off your phone. Believe it or not, the store will be able to function without you for 30-60 minutes.

Go somewhere peaceful, or at the very least, a place that has nothing to do with your type of business. Do something just for you. Sit under a tree and listen to the wind. Read a book. People watch. Whatever makes you feel good.

By giving yourself a real break and change your environment, you'll find yourself rejuvenated and better able to handle the rest of your day when you get back to the store.

Parent and Manager

Go to the people. Learn from them. Live with them. Start with what they know. Build with what they have. The best of leaders when the job is done, when the task is accomplished, the people will say we have done it ourselves. ~ Lao Tzu

Over the years, I've found it very interesting to note how management and rearing children have similar principles.

I remember a fellow trainer telling a story about her daughter, to make a point about guidance. She had asked her daughter, who was relatively young at the time, to clean her playroom. About an hour later, she came back to find her daughter sitting in the middle of the room with nothing done. When she asked why she was just sitting there, her daughter burst into tears and told her she didn't know where to start. She was completely overwhelmed by the magnitude of what she'd been asked to do.

It's important to remember not everybody has the ability to figure out how to get from A to Z. As a leader, it's most likely one of your key skills, probably so second nature; you do it without even realizing it. This is your reminder that not everyone gets it. People don't come to work to do a bad job. The problem is they often don't have the skills necessary to complete what is being asked. As a leader, you must think train and give instruction with a "back to basics" understanding. Think of when you first learned how do to the task and teach it that way.

It's your job to guide and teach the people in your care how to break down the larger tasks into smaller, more attainable ones, to complete the project.

The key is to figure out if your employee is in over his or her head before they start the task. Sending them into an overwhelming situation can be pretty rough on their confidence. You can easily gauge their ability to handle the situation by assigning them the task, and then asking them how they plan to tackle it. If you get a blank stare or panicked stammering, then you know you have a little one-on-one work to do before the task gets started.

This will create happier, more confident staff members; and for those of you who are parents, this approach will help with your children's happiness and confidence too!

The 10% Rule

The conventional definition of management is getting work done through people, but real management is developing people through work. ~ Agha Hasan Abedi

More often than not, we learn what we do not want to be a leader by working with managers who aren't really that good at their jobs.

A friend and colleague told me about a bad experience she'd had with a manager that had a huge impact on her career. Each month the displays that faced into the centre aisle were rotated. He'd asked her to build all the new displays that had come in for the month. She was really excited to do it. She took a lot of time and care to make them look perfect. Hours later, she finished the task, and was very pleased with what she had accomplished. She anticipated the pleasure her manager would convey when he saw the great wonder of what she'd done.

He walked onto the floor, looked down the centre aisle and told her she'd done it all wrong and she would have to do it again, then walked away.

You can imagine how deflating that was.

She vowed never to be that kind of leader, and she adopted a 10% rule. Anytime she set a task for a staff member, she asked them to come and get her when the task was 10% complete. As a retail leader, she knew she was busy, and putting the onus on the staff member to come and get her meant she wouldn't forget to do any coaching that was necessary. It also gave them an added sense of responsibility, and prevented her from breathing over their shoulders. When they came to her, she would look at what had been completed, and then give guidance where it was needed. It also allowed her to give positive reinforcement at the same time.

The 10% Rule allows you to coach with your staff in the early stages of the project, and make any necessary changes before they get too far in. It gets the task done the right way, the first time, and builds understanding and confidence in the employee. That's a win-win situation all around.

Inspire

Ask your staff members for a quote, a song, or the title of a book that really inspires them.

Not only will you get an insight into what is meaningful to each person on your team, you might also find a few things that inspire you. You will always get a better understanding as to how to inspire your staff when they need a little extra motivation!

An inspired staff creates magic.

Let Them See You Sweat

Not the cry, but the flight of a wild duck, leads the flock to fly and follow. ~ Chinese Proverb

A friend of mine told me a story about an owner of a multimillion-dollar wholesale company who would go down to his warehouse every week to sweep the floors. He strongly credited his success to this simple chore because it kept his head in the game. While he was sweeping, he watched what was happening. He learned firsthand how things were going. He could see how his team was working together, what they were accomplishing, and where they had challenges or a need for improvement. Sweeping that floor gave him the ability to stay in touch in a way that he never could, if he stayed in his office and had someone give him a report.

More importantly, his employees saw that he was willing to work as hard as they did, and he wasn't above doing any menial jobs. In other words, he's would do any of the tasks he assigned to them.

The message stuck with me and I believe this is an important lesson for every leader. You need to be willing to get in there and clean the toilets or put away stock when you have to. Doing so, shows you're actually willing to walk the walk, and not just talk the talk. Your team will respect you more for it, become more committed to supporting you as you support them, and they'll know they can count on you to help get the job done.

Be the leader they can rely on in every way.

The Best Players Don't Always Make the Best Coaches

A player who makes a team great is better than a great player. ~ John Wooden

All too often, we promote our best sales people into management positions because they're good at what they do. Then we watch as they struggle, and sometimes crash and burn, simply because they're unable to teach others how to do the things they do.

Think back to school. You had some teachers that were okay, but there were a few teachers that (hopefully) inspired you. They were the ones that helped you to get the most out of your education. These are the same qualities you're looking for in a supervisor or leader.

Rather than promoting someone and then realizing the person is not qualified to do the position, start teaching him or her to do the tasks of a supervisor a little at a time. As they complete and excel at one task, add another, and another. They will either be able to handle the duties and easily step into the management role, or you will learn quickly that this person's skills are better suited to sticking to what they know/do best. Every person has his or her place in making your team successful.

Where's Your Emphasis?

The trick is in what one emphasizes. We either make ourselves miserable, or we make ourselves strong. The amount of work is the same. ~ Carlos Castaneda

What are the things you do to make you strong?

Staff Meetings

Staff meetings should always be inspiring for your staff. The Big Show doesn't stop just because there isn't a customer in the store. The staff meeting is *the* place to make your team feel important. Do that by celebrating your staff's achievements, welcoming new staff members, learning about new products or systems, and working on team building, among other things.

They are never ever a place to correct behaviour. Let me say that again. They are ***never ever*** a place to correct behaviour. Even if your entire team is doing something incorrectly, you should never address it to the group in a staff meeting. Corrections or discipline should always be given directly and personally, on a one-on-one basis. This will give the person who is being corrected the ability to ask questions, and learn at their own pace.

I will say that if your entire team is doing something incorrectly, a staff meeting is a great time to hold a ***training*** session. Training, when done properly, is fun and positive. Hearing that you are doing things wrong is neither fun nor motivating.

Staff meetings should always be scheduled with as much notice as possible. At minimum, you should give a week's notice. You should also post an itinerary of events, so that everyone can be prepared.

There are a few areas that should be covered in every staff meeting.

- Thank everyone for coming
- Welcome new staff members
- Celebrate sales achievements of your superstars
- Announce any staff promotions into new positions
- Share your sales standings and goals
- Provide an outline of the plans to achieve current goals
- Provide an outline of any upcoming sales promotions
- Talk about any new products or discontinued products
- Hold a product knowledge session, including training if required

- Include something fun, like a game that focuses on team building

Staff meetings should be as short and sweet as possible, out of respect for your team members' time. Limit your meetings to a 60-minute maximum whenever possible.

Part of creating the Show means looking for ways to get your team involved in the meeting. It's not something you have to do completely on your own. The more you get people involved in staff meetings, the more they will feel like they are an important part of your store. That's an important ingredient that goes into the magical recipe.

Be Ready

When opportunity comes, it's too late to prepare. ~ John Wooden

Great leaders continue to learn and develop, so they can be even greater leaders. Further your development by reading books on leadership, taking courses to expand your knowledge, studying other great leaders, and then put things you learn into practice. Every time you do, you become more valuable to the people around you, and you'll be more prepared for any opportunity or situation when it arises.

Make a Leadership Moment

Go to a bookstore. Select a book on leadership. Open it to a random page. You're bound to learn something new, connect with a quote, or reaffirm your own belief in leadership. If you don't connect with something on one page, pick up another book and try again. Try this over a week, taking just a few minutes each day to learn something new, and watch how much you'll grow.

It's Not Easy Being Green

Remember, the grass is greener where you water it.

Whether it's you, your business, or the people around you, how are you making the grass greener on your side of the fence?

Schedule Time

It's not the load that breaks you down, it's the way you carry it. ~ Lou Holtz

My physiotherapist is very big on having his clients email him about their progress. For him, it's a measure of how much they're actually interested in doing the work they need to do. That, in and of itself, is a great lesson, but not the one I'm going for right now. When you email him, you get an auto response that says he checks his messages at 2pm and at 9pm, and will respond to the email at that time. When I asked him about it, he said this little step helped him to be much more efficient throughout his workday. By simply scheduling time to return his emails, he was able to give his full attention to his clients while they were with him, and the responses he was able to write when he returned the emails were much more detailed. This was obviously better for his clients all around not to mention that it created a more relaxing situation for him too. He was able to completely focus on the task he was doing at the time, rather than being distracted by something else.

As an added bonus, scheduling time to return emails, and communicating this to his clients, he let them know exactly when they would receive a response, allowing them the same courtesy and ability to focus on their day.

Try adopting the same practice. Unless it's an emergency, have your staff take phone messages for you. Teach them to communicate the times you will respond to the message. The same goes for your email. You too will find that you're more focused and more productive throughout the day, allowing you to do what you need to in order to create the experience you are going for with the Big Show.

Be Fully Present

I admire my sister for many reasons, and her ability to being fully present is just one of them. When she meets with someone at work, she is totally and completely present for him or her, whether it's a client or co-worker. She gives them the respect they deserve, by turning off her cell phone, putting her desk phone on "do not disturb," and by closing her laptop. With no distractions, she is fully focused on the individual for the full time of the meeting. When someone pops into her office without an appointment, and she is too busy to meet with them at that time, she lets him or her know she cannot give them her full attention presently, and then books an appointment, so that she can.

I believe that conveys a great message. It shows she respects them, their time, and all that they have to offer.

Remember, when you're with someone, each time you check your phone, Twitter messages, emails, Facebook page, and so on, you're telling that person that whatever you are doing is much more important than they are. Give the people around you the respect they deserve, and be fully present when they've taken the time to seek you out.

Shhh…Listen

One of the keys in being a great communicator is being a great listener. Truly listening shows you care about what the person is saying. When you're thinking more about what you're going to say, you are not listening. Put your own thoughts aside, and focus on the person in front of you. They are talking with you for a reason. Listen, so you can find out what it is.

In his book, "Who Will Cry When You Die?" Robin Sharma gives pointers to improve your listening skills. Below is a simple paraphrase for you.

1. If you are speaking, and the other person hasn't said anything for more than 60 seconds, you've probably lost them. Stop talking.
2. Resist interrupting. Remember, it's not about what you want to say; it's about what the other person is currently saying.
3. If it's appropriate, take notes. It shows you're truly interested, and that what they have to say is important.
4. After they have made their points, follow up with a question like, "Just to make sure I understand you, are you saying…?" That way, you will make sure you've got it right.

And I'm going to add in one from my sister.

5. Be present, and give them your full attention. Turn off anything that might be a distraction, so you can completely focus on the human being in front of you.

Great communication takes some work. Being aware of your listening skills is the first step.

Create a Peer Network

Get to know other retail leaders from all types of businesses. Whether they sell shoes, pets, electronics or heavy machinery, it's a sure bet that they're going through, have already gone through, or will go through any situation in which you find yourself.

Other retail leaders will understand exactly how you feel. They'll have creative ideas to share with you and vice versa. You can help each other solve problems, or prevent them, by contributing your collective experiences.

A peer group will be able to give you advice that's helpful and effective, because they row exactly the same kind of boat you do.

The Elite Coach

Leading others to reach their own greatness starts by looking inwards, then trusting your team with their unique individual talents.

The Elite Coach

In any leadership position, the most important aspect of your job will be getting your team to work together. The underlying theme of teamwork will be your ability to convey a renewed sense of optimism. Your role as the captain will give the ship direction, purpose and ultimately success. ~ Dale Brown, former basketball coach of the LSU Tigers

As a retail leader, to make the best of your players, you have to be the best coach you can be. The best way to learn those skills is to study the behaviours of the best coaches in the world, whether it's in business or sports. The best coaches get the most out of their players in a number of ways. First, the coach has to know just about all there is to know about the game. He has to know the rules, the plays, the fields or arenas, and the mechanics that go into every aspect of each position, as well as how the positions work together to create a cohesive force. The best coaches also know the areas of expertise that are truly their own, and other areas that are best covered by another coach.

To lead the Big Show, you have to view your position the same way. You have to know the mechanics of the great sale in order to be able to coach on it. You have to understand the operations of the store. Your product knowledge must be extensive. You are the person that has the answers for your team. As the ringleader, you really must have the greatest amount of knowledge in all areas, but that's not to say you have to be *the* expert in every one. After all, the leader of the centre ring isn't the lion-tamer, acrobat and clown. He is there to make sure the show flows with perfection. He ensures they are always getting better, so that each person in the audience receives an experience like no other, every single time. Understanding that someone on your coaching team might serve the team better in a particular area, means you must have the presence of mind to know when to step back, and let someone else take over that part the game. Finding other coaches to enhance the gaps in your own skill set will go a long way to creating a winning team.

The team itself is the next coaching priority. The coaches select the best players they can find to benefit the team. Sometimes, that means bringing in new drafts and trading other players to a different team. They continually evaluate the performance of each person and each position. The starting line-up consists of the best players for each spot, but that doesn't always mean the best players play together on the same line. Elite coaches also know that certain combinations create greater synergy. They evaluate the dynamics of the players, choose the ones that work best together, and then create their lines from there. You can probably think of a couple of people on your team that, when paired together, drive each other's performances to greater heights, but when working with others, they seem flat and tend to underperform. It's knowing that synergy and continually evaluating the performance that perfects the line-up. You need the confidence of the professional sport coaches who aren't afraid to get rid of the players that aren't working for the team, and bring in fresh ones to up the performance.

Coaches continually give feedback to improve each player's performance. They're always looking for the slightest change that can make a big overall difference. Perfecting technique is of the utmost importance because in the middle of the game the player can't be thinking about what he or she has to do next. It has to be as natural as taking the next breath. The only way the player can truly know what he or she has to change is through feedback from the coach, who is continually watching the player's movement, and the development of the play. The player is then given feedback about improvement for particular techniques, or how the player could have adjusted to the play, to be more effective. You have to give your retail team the same advantages. You have to continually watch their performance on the sales floor, and encourage when they do it right, or tweak it when they need a little help. Don't be afraid to give feedback. Getting feedback is the only way your players can ever hope to get better at what they do.

Elite coaches always move the bar higher. Setting greater expectations and higher goals keeps the team striving upward. But the best coaches also know that those expectations can't be met without the right support in place for the players. That might come in the form of training, personal guidance, or encouragement. The coaches know when to push and when to ease back a little. They know which of the team members need gentle coaching, and which need to be kicked in the butt to get going. No matter what, the elite coaches always push their players harder than the players would probably do for themselves, leading them towards greater accountability.

World-class coaches hold their players accountable for their actions. If they aren't going to do the work, they aren't going to get to play. Accountability is of the utmost importance for the team. Everyone has to be measured by the same yardstick in order to keep harmony and keep the team functioning at its best. Without accountability, the team has less cohesion, because everyone is doing what they see fit, and that doesn't always work well with the plans of the player next to them, who is also doing what they see fit.

There is a reason a coach has the position of the leader and runs the show. The coach creates the structure and sees the bigger picture. The coach knows how best to get the separate parts working together to create a more efficient whole. The coach keeps the team moving in the same direction. The coach's word is law and if you want to play the game, you have to do it his or her way. On your team, it's no different. If you want to be the best, you have to hold your team accountable to the rules you have in place. The players that don't want to follow the coach's rules ride the bench, and eventually catch the next bus to elsewhere. You lead your team for one reason: you are the best leader for the team you've created.

Please and Thank You, Thank You, Thank You

I was ordering my coffee, when the barista asked me if I would like some cinnamon on top. I said, "Yes, please. That would be lovely."

She told me how nice it was that I had said please. How incredible is that? She must serve hundreds of people in a day in her busy shop, and she was surprised to hear someone use such a common courtesy, when it should be something that happens all the time.

It begs the question: do you have that kind of courtesy in your store?

Saying please and thank you for doing any kind of task shows appreciation. When your staff have that kind of appreciation, they feel better about themselves and their jobs. And of course, they will view you in a better light too.

More importantly, that kind of courtesy needs to translate down to your customers. Coach your staff to thank your customers for their purchase, or just for simply coming into your store. Look for ways to be courteous in all you do. Hold the door open when they come in or leave, greet them, and ask them to come back to see you again. Remember, your customers have a lot of choices out there when it comes to buying. They don't need to come to your store, but *you* want them there, and making them feel appreciated will go a long way to keep them coming back.

Hello?

Greeting your customers is the first step in excellent customer service, but it has to be a sincere greeting with eye contact. It can't be that disembodied voice coming from underneath the counter...like the ones I used to hear at an unnamed movie rental outlet before they died a great death. I always wanted to wave my hand in front of the door chime to make it go off over and over again to see how many times I could get them to say hello in a row, before they figured it out and climbed out from whatever they were doing under that mysterious counter.

Greeting your customers welcomes them into the store. It lets them know they've been noticed, and they also know that there is *at least one* person they can go to if they need help. And as an added bonus, it's been shown that if you make eye contact and talk to a would-be thief, that person is much less likely to steal from you. You can't beat that.

Get to Know Your Staff

A good manager is a man who isn't worried about his own career, but rather the careers of those who work for him. ~ H S M Burns

My first three months as a manager in a big box store were completely overwhelming for me. There were so many balls to juggle, between the operations of the store and hitting the sales targets that were expected, that I had blinders on to just about everything else going on, just so I could make it through the day without losing my mind.

That was the case until my new assistant manager pulled me aside and asked me what the heck I was doing. Actually, she used much more colourful words, and took a lot longer to say it, but you get the drift.

Of course, I had absolutely no idea what she was talking about. Then, she laid it out pretty succinctly. I had walked from the front to the back of the store, focused on whatever task I was doing. On the way, I had passed several of my staff members and hadn't even bothered to acknowledge them. Moreover, I didn't know a darn (insert appropriate expletive here) thing about any of my staff members, and I would never be able to develop any type of team if I wasn't going to bother being a part of it.

I was completely shocked. Worse, I knew she was completely right and I had to change immediately to become the leader that I wanted to be.

As a leader you have to get to know your staff. Learn what makes them tick, what motivates them, what their aspirations and inspirations are, and so on. You have to show up and show them that you care. When you have that, your staff will be much more likely to go to the wall for you during those times when you need the extra help. It will also make them happier to come to work each day.

I still cringe when I think about how awful it was for the staff members who stuck it out with me through those first few months. Of course, it did take many more months to get it going in the right direction, but at least after that "chat," it did get better for everyone, myself included.

When you do take the time to get to know your staff, you have to bear in mind that there needs to be a balance between the personal and the professional. You are their leader, not their best friend. Unless you have a very rare team, you can't go out, party with them, and expect them not to take it personally when you have to call them on unacceptable behaviours at the store level. People aren't usually made that way and they have a difficult time making that separation.

Not only that, but you have to keep your own feelings in check. When you get too close, it's easier to make excuses for unacceptable behaviour.

Sally just broke up with her boyfriend, so I can understand why she isn't helping as many people as she usually does. Joe is under a lot of pressure with exams this week, so I'm not going to talk to him about his poor sales right now.

When you get too close, it's too easy to excuse poor performance. You must always keep in mind that you are running a business and that the business has to come first.

You have to trust in yourself to find the right balance. Take a little personal time to chat with each of your staff members before their shift starts. Learn about them and connect. Then get down to business once it's time to hit the floor.

Turn that Frown Upside Down

Once you replace negative thoughts with positive ones, you'll start having positive results. ~ Willie Nelson

We all have bad days; those days where you just wake up, and it's not going well right from the moment your eyes open. Of course, as a leader in retail, you can't afford to have a bad day because your staff and your customers will definitely pick up on it. And the thing about a bad day is that it spreads like the common cold in a day care centre – you parents know exactly what I'm talking about!

The thing to do is to cut it off before it really wears you down. It's not easy to do, and everyone has their own ways of coping. However, if you ever get really stuck, here are a few things that work to bring you to a better frame of mind:

1. Stand tall. It's been shown that standing up straighter not only helps your posture, it can also make you feel more positive. If nothing else, you'll look more confident; and when you look it, you feel it.

2. Smile. It reduces stress and lowers your blood pressure. And smiles are contagious. Before you know it, the whole store will be smiling right along with you!

3. Give five people in your store a *sincere* compliment. Making someone else feel good will help to make you feel better too.

4. Blast your playlist of "happy music" to get your mojo going. I have a list that my husband made for me, called "Dance, Andy Dance." Just the name of it makes me happy before I push the play button.

5. Adopt the "fake it till you make it" attitude. Act like you're happy, and chances are you'll be feeling that way before you know it.

6. Finally, telling a good joke can help too. And if you don't know one to share, try this…

   My friend told me the only food that can make you cry is an onion, so I threw a coconut at his face.

   Makes me laugh every time.

Being Grateful

A man's life is what his thoughts make of it. ~ Marcus Aurelius

I have a friend who writes down 10 things he's grateful for each month, then reads them each morning before work. Others I know have a "grateful journal" that they write in every night and read from when they are feeling particularly stressed. By doing so, it helps them to focus on the things that are truly important in their lives.

What are you grateful for?

Hello, Thank You, Goodbye

In many South American and European cultures, it's appropriate to go around and say hello to every person who works for you before you start your day. Then before leaving at the end of day, it's also customary to shake everybody's hand and thank them for the work they've done during the day. This is done for each and every member of the team, every single day.

I love this concept. It's such a small thing, but has potentially big results.

Imagine how important it must make each person feel to have their boss greet them, and then also thank them for the work they've done. Every day!

Imagine how good you would feel making each person on your team smile and feel appreciated. Just by saying hello, thank you, and goodbye.

Now stop imagining it and do it.

Schedule Worry Time

No problem can withstand the assault of sustained thinking. ~ Voltaire

In times of particular stress, sit down with a pen and a pad of paper, and write down everything that's worrying you. It doesn't matter what it is, rational or not, just write it down. When you do, you'll find there is much on your mind that is static stress, or something you can't do anything about. Those are the "what if" worries.

"What if the bus comes late?" "What if my child gets hurt?" "What if my spouse has an accident?".

These "what ifs" are endless and are all very normal worries that we all have. Give yourself 20 minutes to worry over it, and then set it aside. If you do this regularly, you will find these things will have less power in your life. Let's face it, much of it will never happen and if it does happen, you will do what you have to do to work through it, at that time. There is no point in letting these "what ifs" paralyze the life you are living now.

There will be some worries on your list that perhaps need an outside perspective. Write down the name of the person that can most likely help you solve the issue and contact them.

Finally, the last of the worries you have listed probably have solutions you can easily work out. Write down the solutions as you see them, and make a plan of action. Then, get it done.

Writing down your worries can be a constructive exercise that gives them voice, and helps you recognize you have options to make things better. You will also recognize the things that are simply wasting your precious time.

You Did it!

Catch someone doing something right. ~ Kenneth Blanchard and Spencer Johnson

Then let them know they did it right! It will make you and your team happier for doing it.

Positive Thinking

The positive thinker sees the invisible, feels the intangible, and achieves the impossible. ~ Author Unknown

Our internal dialogue has a very big affect on our own confidence. Unfortunately, we often spend a lot of time beating ourselves up and filling our own minds with self-doubt. There is only one person who can make that change in your life. Can you guess who? I'll give you a hint: they're reading this book right now.

A business coach I know suggests to his clients to write down a list of personally positive "I am" statements. Statements such as:

> I am creative.

> I am confident.

> I am a great parent.

> I am a leader.

Each night they are to read them before they go to bed, ending each day on a positive personal note. During times when they feel less than confident, he tells them to pull out the list and focus on the reality of who they actually are. Small changes over time will make large personal gains in the long run.

Your challenge should you accept to take it:

Start with 10 positive "I am" statements. Read them before you go to sleep or a week, and then build from there.

Just a Little Change...

Today, take a look at your work systems and processes. Change one thing to make it better.

One small change can make an amazingly big impact to your efficiency and productivity.

Knowing Your Strengths...and Where to Improve

Surround yourself with the best people you can find, delegate authority, and don't interfere as long as the policy you've decided upon is being carried out. ~ Ronald Reagan

We all have things at which we excel in our careers and we have things that aren't quite our forte.

Write down five things you do well. Take a moment to celebrate it. It's always important to appreciate yourself.

Now write three things you find challenging.

Remember, you are human. You can't do it all. In fact, if you to do it all, you will most assuredly fail. A one-man circus would be a poor show indeed. Give yourself permission to let go of these challenging things. You will be much more effective by focusing on the things *you do* best. Those things are the reason you are where you are and why you are most effective with them.

Now consider your team. Who will excel at doing the tasks you find challenging? Who can further their career by taking on these extra responsibilities? Who will appreciate and be empowered by doing these things?

A great leader finds the people who complement his or her abilities. It gives you both the opportunity to achieve more. Together, it creates balance, synergy and strength. That's what the Big Show is all about, creating an experience of "more," both for your clients and for you team.

Teach them and watch them fly.

Do You Need a Bath?

People often say that motivation doesn't last. Well, neither does bathing – that's why we recommend it daily. ~ Zig Ziglar

Motivation is a bath for your determination. Run that water.

Fish!

Watching the workers at the world famous Pikes Place Fish Market is an awesome experience and a lesson in excellent customer service. It perfectly exemplifies the Big Show. If you've been there, you know exactly what I'm talking about. Slinging fish for a living didn't sound like a lot of fun to me, but seeing the guys in action was a great thing. Every interaction was something to watch. They enjoyed each other, they interacted with a lot of customers, they made a lot of people smile, and *they sold a lot* of fish.

So just who are they? They are Stephen C. Lundin, Harry Paul, John Christensen, ad Kevin Blanchford. AND, they are so good at what they do, that they wrote a book about it called *Fish! A Proven Way to Boost Morale and Improve Results*, and made a video about it too. In it they talk about five different principals they use that can boost morale in any business. My favourite is "Choose Your Attitude" because attitude is absolutely a choice.

How you react to any given situation is a choice. Becoming angry and losing your temper, or choosing to be calm and recognizing you have the ability to make a bad situation better, is a choice you can make within yourself during times of adversity. You can choose to have a good day or a bad day. You can choose to let traffic get you down or not. You can choose to react to a situation in whatever way you want.

Does it take some practice? Absolutely. Yet, once you choose to focus on it, it becomes easier to make the change.

Choose to get the book or watch their video. Choose to share it with your staff. Choose to make a difference for yourself and your team.

Create Wins

Coaches who can outline plays on a black board are a dime a dozen. The coaches who win are the ones who can motivate their players. ~ Vince Lombardi

I overheard one of my supervisors coaching with a brand new hire. This was her very first job and sales position. He pointed out an older gentleman in the store. Her mission was to go talk to him and find out if he had grandchildren, and, if so, how many he had. She was to come back and report to him after she found out.

I thought that was absolutely brilliant.

One of the first things a great sales person has to do is start a conversation out of nothing and be comfortable doing it. He was slowly teaching her to do that by giving her a topic and showing her she could do it, without having any pressure to make a sale.

Baby steps are the start to making bigger strides.

Elementary, My Dear Watson

The best teams have chemistry. They communicate with each other and they sacrifice personal glory for the common goal. ~ Dave DeBusschere

How's the communication in your team? Are you all striving for a common goal? Does everyone know what's important?

All great questions that need to be answered. And the question that follows each one: What is the evidence to show it?

Without concrete evidence, you just don't know.

Bench Strength

Behind an able man there are always other able men. ~ Chinese Proverb

Any sports coach will tell you that having an abundance of talent to choose from is a wonderful thing and a true gift. The team that can pick from any of the players on the bench and come up with a strong line is going to have a much easier time getting to the championship rounds. They will be better rested and more mentally fit because they haven't exhausted themselves to get to the finish. They will win as a team working together.

I love the quote by Knute Rockne, an American football player and coach: **"As a coach, I play not my eleven best, but my best eleven."** He can only do that when there are more skilled and competent people to choose from on any given day.

Your management team needs to be that bench strength for you. Whether you're away from the store, having an off day, or just needing extra support, it's the team around you that will save you. If they aren't strong enough, you will be carrying the weight all on your own, and sooner or later that weight will sink you.

I've had many managers who worried that their assistant manager might outshine them. So what? It doesn't make you look bad, it makes you look great! It's a compliment to your skills of choosing the right person and teaching them what they need to know to excel. Having a team around you that shines, shows you know what you're doing. You put them there.

Think of how much easier your life will be, when you have a person you can rely on to take some of the duties that are weighing you down. It would free up some of that time you're spending doing things you don't really need to do. It would let you get on with being the leader you can be. You could focus on developing the areas that make you a great leader, while the other people on your team develop the areas that are their strengths. And then if together, as a team, you could develop the staff underneath you to do the same thing, how easy would it be to achieve your goals?

Now take a look at it from you company's standpoint. The leader who can consistently develop an entire team to exceed the goals set for them is much more valuable. That leader could then develop more leaders to do the same thing, and the company will get stronger. That means the Big Show gets to go far beyond your single location.

It's like building a card pyramid. The only way you can make that one on top balance is to create a strong base that won't waver, as you build the upper levels. Add in some super glue and you've got it made.

Now, you just have to recognize that super glue is *you*.

Micromanagement

Never tell people how to do things. Tell them what to do and they will surprise you with their ingenuity. ~ George Patton

I personally find micromanagers the most difficult people to deal with, and I am sure there are many other people out there like me. I'm a strong personality, and I like to share ideas; and I think therein lies the rub with the micromanager.

Micromanagement is one-way communication. I use communication in its broadest sense here, because I believe real communication is like a tennis match. It goes back and forth between at least two people. Micromanagement, however, is just one person imposing their ideals without room for anything else from anyone else. You can't create any magic with that.

Micromanagement happens when a leader obsessively controls every aspect of the task being completed. For example, if you were washing the dishes, a micromanager would be standing by, telling you how hot the water should be, how full the sink should get, how much soap to use, what order the dishes should be washed, how they should be rinsed...you probably get the picture. This management style is so controlled that they might just as well do it themselves.

I will agree that there are times that someone will need more hands-on guidance; but I am sure *you* will agree, there is a big difference between guidance and micromanagement.

Think back to your greatest achievements, or the times in your life when you've learned the most. I'll bet that during those times, you learned a lot from your mistakes. Getting it wrong allows you to learn how to do it right. Micromanagement stops that kind of growth, because it never allows for it. No one is allowed to think or act on his or her own judgement. So how can growth truly happen?

Micromanagement also stifles creativity and change. When someone is standing over you to tell you how to complete every detail of a task, there is no thinking for yourself. There are no thoughts on ways to make it better. Failure allows you to take a look at the system, and see what you can to do change it, adapt it, and make it more efficient.

As the opening quote of this section says, let people use their own ingenuity to find a solution to what needs to be done.

Experience that Matters

The golden rule for every businessman is this: "Put yourself in your customer's place." – Orison Swett Marden

Your customers' experience in your store will have a huge influence on whether or not they will continue to buy from you. They are the reason you are creating the Big Show. Their experience means everything. That experience covers everything from the cleanliness of your store and how well it's priced, to how nicely they are treated by your staff, and how long they have to wait in the cash line-up. The nice thing is that all of these factors are under your control.

Put yourself in your customer's shoes, and no doubt you'll come up with a few things you can do to make your store even better.

Alter the Road to Hell

There are some people you will "click" with as soon as you meet them, others that you like and work well with, and still others that you might immediately dislike, or through a set of circumstances, come to dislike. That's a reality of life. In your role as a retail leader, you work with all these types of people. I'm sure you can bring to mind one or two people who fit into each of these particular categories right now.

Think about going into a meeting with one of the people that you really "click" with and like a lot. Focus on how you feel at the thought of meeting with that person. You might pick words like happy, good, energized or cheerful. You know that no matter what you have to say, it's going to be a good conversation, because you get along with that particular person. This person makes you feel good.

Now, think about going into a meeting with a person that you really dislike. Your feelings have probably done a complete turnaround. Perhaps now you feel anxious, angry, upset or uneasy. You can imagine that this conversation will be a battle from start to finish. You can probably even plot out how the conversation will go. "When he says that, then I will say this." You can probably feel your blood start to boil, just thinking about this imaginary meeting.

The question to ask is, "How much of this is a self-fulfilling prophecy?"

You know that when you meet with the person you like, you're going to feel good. You've already decided how the meeting will end, so you go into the meeting with the expectation of a positive outcome. Every action you take will support the fact that you like the person, and you're happy to see them. Therefore, you will get exactly what you thought you would get out of the meeting.

Conversely, haven't you done exactly the same thing with the person you dislike? You've decided the meeting isn't going to go well, so it doesn't because you're already focusing on the things that will make it go badly. You enter the meeting, purposefully looking for faults in the other person that you know will be there; naturally finding them, proving yourself right. Your actions mirror your thoughts, and you end up getting the poor results that you expected to get.

What would happen if you decided that the meeting with the person you don't like was going to go well? You set yourself the intention that this is going to be a great meeting and that there will be a positive outcome. Decide that you will recognize some of the good qualities this person has and that you will work to connect with those qualities. How are you feeling inside now? Maybe a little less anxious or angry? Won't that alone have a more positive effect on the meeting?

Recognize that there are times when you set yourself up to get exactly what you intend to get out of a meeting, good or bad. Change your intention, and you will get different results.

Concrete Coaching

I've heard many a friend tell a story about how they were compared to their brother or sister when they were growing up. The worst of all comparisons was, "Why can't you be more like…?" It caused resentment and rightly so, because that person is completely different from their brother or sister and should be judged on their own merits or mistakes.

Take that to heart when you coach with your team. You can't create the environment for the Big Show if you set up this kind of negativity. Comparing anyone on your team to another will only build resentment and discontent. Anytime you coach with someone on your team, you must use hard data to back up what you're saying. Focus on the individual you are coaching, not their peers.

Think about a basketball player standing on the free throw line. From the bench, the coach is watching how his or her body moves when the shot is lined up, and if the shot is missed, the coach can give feedback to make it better. Line up the hips to be square with the basket; bend at the knees; focus on the back of the rim; line up the arm with the basket; take a deep breath to settle; follow through with the hand as the shot is made. THIS is hard data to analyze. It's objective data. Missing any one of those steps can make the shot go awry. The coach can now tell the player which of the steps needs to be worked on, in order to make the shot the next time.

Sales coaching must be treated the same way. You have to use hard facts that, when changed or adjusted, will produce the results you want. The person either greeted the customer or they didn't, added onto the sale or not, met their sales goal or missed it. It has to be black and white, with no room for argument as to whether or not the behaviour happened. There is nothing subjective about it. There is no "I think" this happened. It's a hard fact that it did happen.

Similarly, the coaching you give to improve an issue has to be concrete as well. You can't just tell them to make their sales better. You have to give them specific ways to do it. In the instance that a person didn't add on to the sale, the problem could be that they don't really know what they should suggest to go with the product purchased. That means specific product training would be necessary.

Let's say for example that our sales person, Joel, just sold a person a pair of designer suede boots, in a city that uses salt on the sidewalks in the wintertime. An excellent add-on to the sale would be a product to protect the boots against salt. If Joel learns about the product and other products like it, he will be able to inform the customer, and attempt to add it on to the purchase. The more he knows about the product, the more educated and confident he will be, and the more likely it is that the customer will purchase it. That's concrete coaching.

Think about the ways you can improve your coaching by using specific and concrete data.

Money Talk

Strategically using the numbers to your advantage.

The Value of a Sharpie®

It's important to understand the true cost of the supplies necessary for running your store every day. Controlling your business expenses is a key factor in having a strong bottom line.

There were so many times, as a manager, when I couldn't find a pen or a marker when I needed one. Inevitably, it meant that I went to the office to pull out another one.

You need to note as a retail leader that those migrating pens, pencils, markers and Sharpies® cost your business money when you have to replace them. Most people recognize that it is an expense, but don't really think about the true cost to the company. What you need to consider is the amount of sales it takes to generate enough income to replace each Sharpie® that goes missing. Every expense needs a generation of revenue to pay for it.

Don't believe me? Time for some fun:

Let's say the Sharpie® costs $1.97. And let's say you're operating at a 5% bottom line profit margin.

$1.97 (cost)/ 5% (bottom line profit margin) = $39.40

That's how much you have to generate in sales to break even every time you have to replace a Sharpie®. Add the $1.97 cost for the original Sharpie® and the true value of the new replacement is $41.37. That means replacing a Sharpie® on a weekly basis costs your business $2,151.24 over the course of a year. And that's straight off your bottom line profit.

Rather eye opening, isn't it? I don't know about you, but I could put that money to much better use in business.

Take a good look at your controllable operational costs. Where else are you needlessly losing money?

Covet thy pens, pencils, markers and Sharpies®.

Dana White

A lot can be learned from watching leaders in other businesses. When you want to create the Big Show, the person to study is Dana White. I am personally in awe of him and the things he's accomplished with the UFC (Ultimate Fighting Championship). He runs a tight ship. He is always looking for ways to make it bigger and better. He keeps his fighters in line. And above all, he engages the fans in a variety of ways.

One of the things he does before each major bout is a ticket giveaway. What I like about it is the way he does it. He Tweets out his current location in whichever city he is visiting and tells the fans that the first person to come find him gets the tickets.

There are many ways he could give away the tickets, but he chooses to do it in a more personal way. It's a one-on-one meeting with him, bolstered by a fantastic reward that any UFC fan would both covet and appreciate. Absolutely brilliant.

How can you use this? If you have the ability, why not do the same type of thing, but turn it into something of value specific to your customers? Get social media working for you. Tweet out that the next customer that comes up to you and says your store is great, gets a gift card. Announce in your store that the first customer to locate the manager on the floor and tell a good joke gets a surprise gift.

It doesn't matter really what it is, it's more about creating fun, getting your customers personally involved with you, connecting, and most importantly, rewarding their loyalty. It all creates an amazing experience that people come back for time and time again,

Another Perspective

Ask a customer one thing they feel you could do to improve your store. Consider it. If it's feasible, do it.

The best ideas often come from someone not directly involved in your business.

R-E-S-P-E-C-T Through Consistency

You can't demand respect. You have to command it.

The Big Show demands a leader that the team can look to for guidance and trust. Consistency in your behaviours and actions will create better trust. When you are consistent, people know what to expect. Inconsistency undermines trust because they never know what they are going to get, so how can they trust you? Add in fairness, equality and encouraging words, and you will make a supportive environment that people want to work in.

When you put all that together, respect is inevitable.

Conversion Rates

What gets measured gets managed. ~ Peter Drucker

A conversion rate is the percentage of customers that go through the cash register (**Customer Count**) as compared to the number of people that walk through the doors of the store (**Customer Flow**).

Customer Count/Customer Flow = Conversion Rate

If you have a store with a single door, where the customer must enter and exit through the same door, you simply divide your customer flow in half to get the appropriate number to use in the equation.

Tracking your conversion allows you to evaluate the success of your sales team and your store. People come into your store for a reason. Whether the customer is buying something for him or herself, or as a gift for someone else, they do want something you have to offer, or they wouldn't be in your store in the first place. I know I've walked into a store with no real intention of buying anything, but I did go into the store because I liked something they had to offer. I also know that many times, I found something that piqued my interest, and walked out of the store with an unintended purchase in my hands. We've all been there, haven't we? I can honestly say that I've never walked into a store that didn't have something of interest to me, or the person I was shopping with at the time. The stores that are unappealing to me are the stores that I walk by without a second glance.

You and your team decide whether or not to engage the customer that has walked into your store. It's a conscious choice. Your conversion rate is a great indicator of how well you are connecting with each person in your store.

No matter what your conversion rate is, it's a number that you simply want to make better. Turning more of your customers into buyers is a very important aspect in increasing your overall sales numbers.

There could be many reasons that a store's conversion rate is lower than it should be.

- The sales team might not be effectively selling to your customers
- Improper staff scheduling
- A lack of proper product training for your staff
- The products are visually poorly priced
- Ineffective merchandising and display
- Difficulty of store navigation for your customers, no real flow
- A lack of direction and coaching by the team leaders
- Improper hiring practices
- And so on

I'm sure you can think of many other reasons a customer might not buy when walking into a retail outlet.

Evaluating the reason(s) for a poor conversion rate will be individual to each store. There could be more than one factor that's affecting it at the same time. For example, a store that has poor hiring practices and poor training has two very large obstacles to overcome prior to improving the conversion rate. One might argue that putting proper training into place first, would be more effective, but that might depend on whether or not there was someone currently on the team that was good at creating a training program. If not, then the hiring practices might have to be looked at first, in order to hire the right person to develop the training.

Your job as a retail leader is to take a look at what's happening in your store, and then figure out where you need to focus to make your conversion rate better.

Converting through Staff Picks

I often frequent Chapter's because I love books. I have thousands of them on my shelves at home and often think I should start my own little library. However, when at Chapter's, browsing their shelves, the "Staff Picks" displayed often intrigue me. I have no idea who this staff person is most of the time, but I am happy to pick up a book they suggest, and many times buy it. This is part of what goes into making a customer experience worthy of the Big Show: creating points of interest without having to stand there and physically point to it. Chapter's found a way to create their own little spotlight.

Can you find a way adopt a "Staff Picks" program in your store?

Approach the Customer

I had an extra 15 minutes left on my lunch break, so I thought I would stop by a shoe store to see what they had to offer for new work shoes. Now, unlike many women, I hate shopping for shoes. I can never find what I want, when I need it. Or if I find something I like, it doesn't always fit well. It's the curse of big feet and high arches. So inevitably, if/when I find something that works, I immediately buy it.

This specific lunch break impromptu shoe shop, there were two sales people standing side by side. They greeted me in a friendly manner when I walked in, and then continued their work conversation. After a few minutes of browsing, I spied a pair of shoes I thought looked comfortable, and would work with the uniform I had to wear. Not too ugly, while appearing seemingly sturdy and supportive enough for these high arches. I checked my watch, and I still had enough time.

Then the self-doubt started.

If I try these on and they don't fit, I'm going to be disappointed, and that won't make me happy. Of course, if they work, then I don't have to search anymore, and that would make me happy. What do I do?

The doubt won out, I put the shoe back on the shelf and I walked out the door.

About five feet outside the store, it hit me. This was the perfect 'ah ha' moment for me as a manager and trainer, when I was coaching my team on conversion rates and customer service. If either one of the sales people had asked me if I wanted to try on the shoes, I would have said "yes," because deep down, I did really want the shoes.

If the shoes had fit, I would have bought them immediately. They could have made a customer out of me, if they had only bothered to ask if I wanted to try on the shoe I was holding.

The bottom line of this story: talk to your customers after you greet them.

Average Sale

The average sale is calculated when you divide your sales by the number of customers through your cash register.

Sales/Customer Count = Average Sale

The average sale is a direct indicator of how well your sales team is doing in the store. The higher the average sale, the better the store is doing overall. This could mean that your store is effective at selling higher ticket items, or it might mean that your sales team is able to add on extra items to the original purchase, or a healthy combination of both.

It can also indicate how well your sales managers are working the floor. Sales managers that are continually directing your staff to customers, and coaching your sales team to make more effective sales, will create a higher overall average sale for the store. Managers that don't direct their teams and fail to coach properly will consistently have lower average sales. Those sales managers will need coaching from you to become more effective at running the sales floor.

It's important to track both the average sale for the store, and for the individual members of your sales team. It's an excellent tool for coaching. Naturally, by increasing your average sale for each individual on your team, the average sale for the store will also increase, and that, in turn, will increase your overall sales. It makes sense to focus on making it better.

The average sale can be affected in many ways, including:

- Sales training
- Sales coaching
- Product knowledge
- Product mix
- Merchandising
- Pricing

The operational factors, like product mix and variety, merchandising and pricing, will have an effect on the average sale; but hands down, the largest impact will come from making sure your team has the sales knowledge, selling skills and coaching they need to improve and become better at what they do. There is no trade for constant and consistent feedback.

It doesn't matter what your average sale is now, the goal is just to make the number better. Average sale is an excellent statistic to use as a measurement, because it's very easy to see if what you are doing is effective. If the average sale increases with a particular change you've made, then you know you're on the right track. If it doesn't, then it's back to the drawing board to try again.

The Big Show requires attention, analysis, and re-approaching. It's figuring out a way to do it better, even when it's going well. It's a never-ending stream of excellence, all the time.

Product Knowledge

A product knowledge book is a great way to educate your staff on the products you sell in the store. It's very easy to accomplish, with little work on your part. Remember, in order to run the Big Show, you can't do it all, but you do have to oversee it all.

Get your team involved in the process by getting each one to pick a product, and make a product report, highlighting the selling points that would be of service to your customers. Have them include a picture of the product, so it's easier for other members on your team to identify it.

File each product report in a binder, creating a book for your new and existing staff members to quickly learn about some of the awesome products they can offer to their customers based on the customers' needs.

Your Influence as a Sales Leader

A desk is a dangerous place from which to view the world. ~ John Le Caré

I had a supervisor who worked every Wednesday night, which, based on customer flow, was statistically the slowest night of the week. She consistently posted the worst numbers for conversion, average sale, and overall sales on that night, as compared to any other shift during the week. Worse, no matter how good the numbers were when she took over the sales floor, they would drop when she was the leader on the floor. She was okay with this because, in her head, a slow night meant all the numbers would be low, and it made sense that they would drop.

Now, if you're nodding because you think the numbers on the slowest night of the week should be low, keep reading, you don't understand how to create the Big Show yet. And if you don't think they should be low, keep reading anyway, to get affirmation as to why you're right.

On a slow night, the person leading the sales in the Big Show should have a very high conversion rate, since he or she should easily be able to direct one of the sales team to any customer in the store to assist them. With few customers, no one should get missed. As well, it should be easier to connect with the customer and turn them into a buyer, since there would be little distraction for the team to assist other waiting customers.

A great sales leader would also have a very high average sale on a slow night, because each sales person could be coached to take his or her time with each customer. They could really get to know their customers, and have an in-depth discussion about what is needed and why. The sales team should then be easily able to add on to every sale, because they would have a greater understanding of the customers' needs, wants and values.

Based on these criteria, Wednesday nights in her store should actually have the highest conversion and average sale rates of any night of during week, not the lowest.

This supervisor was completely convinced that the numbers she was producing were purely circumstantial. She didn't see that there was anything she could do to improve them.

I was convinced that there was a lot she could do to improve them. She just had to realize her actions could have a big impact.

In order to track her coaching progress, we set up a daily coaching log for her to use. She had to use it every time she was the sales leader, slow day or not, so she could consistently monitor her efforts. In the daily coaching log, she would record the staff members who were working on each shift, and detail the coaching she did with each one of them to improve their individual sales.

She was typically a night manager, so she also had to record the sales statistics of the manager running the floor before her shift, on her daily coaching log. Her objective was to make sure the numbers didn't drop below what she had recorded. From there, she needed to evaluate those statistics, and create sales games she could play with the staff, to make the night a bit more fun and interesting. The sales game had to focus on increasing either the conversion rate or the average sale, based on the one that would have the greatest impact on the overall sales.

We chose a period of four weeks to monitor her progress, and we made a deal. She would give my coaching her best shot during that time, and if she proved to be right, and she didn't affect the numbers, she could go back to her old way of running the floor.

By the end of the second week, she had increased her conversion rates every shift she worked by about 5%, and the average sale by more than 10%, as compared to her previous averages. This was all based on her own historical data.

She was shocked by her success, and how easy it was to affect what was happening in the store. She realized, in that moment, how great a sales leader she could be.

When you and your team understand the impact you can make on *your* sales, you are on your way to the Big Show.

Get Your Customers Involved

As leaders of the Big Show, we are all aware that positively interacting with our customers is important to building trust and loyalty. Many companies use social media to interact on a larger level, but it's the face-to-face interaction that has the greatest impact. Why not make it fun for your customers and your staff members? That makes for a magical experience and that's what the Big Show is all about.

In one company a worked for, one of the most popular cashiers made up trivia questions for the people waiting in the line-up. When someone answered correctly, he gave him or her one of the free giveaways on the counter, that they could take if they wanted. It wasn't actually about the prize; it was about the engagement he created with the customers. They enjoyed standing in his line-up, and had no problem waiting their turn.

You could take fun polls about things that don't really have anything to do with your store, like favourite sports teams, best vacation spots, and so on. You could take it a step further, and ask your customers about your displays, and if they like them, or what they think of your new merchandising, or their thoughts on a new product you have in the store. Direct feedback is excellent to receive from the people you are trying to connect with.

Whatever it is you choose to do, it just has to be fun and engaging for everyone. Create that experience.

Games

A business has to be involving, it has to be fun, and it has to exercise your creative instincts. ~ Richard Branson

The Big Show is an experience for everyone, especially your staff. Playing games to improve sales statistics is a fun and rewarding way to encourage your staff to improve their individual numbers. And friendly competition amongst staff is always a good thing.

The key to creating an effective game lies in choosing to focus on the statistic that will have the greatest impact on your overall sales. As previously mentioned, the two main ones are the conversion rate and the average sale; however, you could also focus on items per sale or sales per hour.

If your conversion rate is low, play a game around increasing each person's individual customer count each hour. That will help to increase the overall conversion rate.

When the focus is on the average sale, you can impact it by selling more large ticket items, or by making more add-on sales. The game then would focus on either one of these areas. It's better to stick to one thing, so everyone is clear on the expectation, rather than trying to challenge both areas at the same time.

Items per sale directly focuses on add-on sales, while an increase in sales per hour can be improved by selling large ticket items, and/or focusing on increasing add-on sales for each person. Again, just make sure your team fully understands where the challenge lies.

I know some retail leaders that have created intensive team games based loosely on the rules of reality shows like CBS' *Survivor* or *The Amazing Race*, while other leaders have created games designed to get different departments working together. It doesn't matter what it is, as long as your team enjoys it, and it helps motivate them to sell more.

Remember to create ways for your cashiers, stock managers, and other team members in non-sales positions to get involved in the game, by setting other goals for them to achieve. It's about encouraging all employees to excel in their positions as well.

If you are unable to buy prizes or give cash prizes, you can offer things like an extra 15 minutes on a break, the choice of a shift on the next schedule, or give a coupon to redeem, that gets them out of doing a task they've been assigned. You can be creative with it.

Here are a few easy game ideas to get you started:

Poker: Deal everyone a card. Each hour they meet or exceed the goal you've set, they get to draw another card. Best hand at the end of the day wins the prize. The more cards they get, the better their chances are to get a winning hand.

Steal the Envelope: Write down several prizes on small sheets of paper, and then enclose each one in separate envelopes. For fun, you can make one of the envelopes a gag prize, or one that contains no prize. The envelopes cannot be opened until the end of the shift, or the end of the game. As your staff meet or exceed the goals you have set, they can select an envelope. Once all the envelopes are in play, the fun begins. Anyone who now meets or exceeds the goals, gets to choose which envelope they will steal from their co-worker. At the end of the game, the people left with the envelopes get to open them and take home the prize.

Hi/Low: The top person wins a prize, and the bottom person has to do a nasty job. For fun, you can challenge your team to collectively beat the goal you've set, and if they do, *you* will do the nasty job. You'd be surprised at how motivated they can be to get their manager to clean a toilet bowl.

The Longest Receipt: This is a great game when you are working to improve add-on sales. Your sales people keep a copy of their register receipts. The person holding the longest one - that isn't a return receipt - at the end of the game wins the prize.

Bingo: Create a bingo card featuring various products from your store. As your staff members sell an item, they mark it off. First one to get a line wins a prize. Or you could play blackout bingo, where they have to fill the whole card. You can end the game when someone wins, or you continue to give rewards as people continue to make lines, until you reach a blackout bingo.

Numbers Don't Lie

I believe the real difference between success and failure in a corporation can be very often traced to the question of how well the organization brings out the great energies and talents of its people. ~ Thomas J. Watson, Jr.

One management team I coached all agreed that "Sally" was the best sales person in the store, hands down. When I checked her sales numbers, she was actually one of the lowest performing sales people in the store. So why did they think she was the best? It was because she worked hard. She showed up on time, she was happy to be at work, she was friendly with the customers, and she did whatever the management team asked her to do, with no fuss. Because of this, they never really bothered to check her sales statistics. They just assumed they were good.

Ironically, the best and most consistent sales person in the store was a young lady that didn't fit well into the store's culture. "Josie" didn't always comply with the uniform standard. She questioned the reasons she was given operational tasks to complete, and punctuality wasn't her strong suit. She was, however, very passionate about her area of expertise in the store, she was very knowledgeable overall about the products, and this translated really well to her customers. However, because she challenged the management team daily, they perceived her to be a bad sales person.

There are, of course, a couple of issues going on here. I'm a big believer in following rules and making people accountable for them. This store obviously needed help with that, but the topic here is the sales numbers. The management team should have been celebrating and acknowledging the amazing sales of their best sales person, Josie. They should also have been coaching with Sally to get her sales numbers up, but their perception was holding them back.

For Sally, two things needed to change. The first was the coaching plan. The management team needed to make one for her. Because she was so compliant, they didn't bother to give her any sales coaching at all. Upon evaluating the tasks Sally was given each shift, the team realized they gave Sally most of the operational duties, because she would complete them with little or no supervision. This was holding her back from helping customers in the store. By sharing the workload with other staff members, Sally was able to help more customers.

Interestingly, when the management team started coaching directly with Sally, she finally told them how happy she was to be able to help more customers. She didn't really like doing all the operational tasks she had been given, but she didn't want to say anything, because she felt the team needed her to do what she was assigned. The coaching made her better at her job, and much happier too.

Incidentally, Josie did better with compliance on the operational issues she was assigned, after she was given more positive reinforcement for her sales, and she was held accountable for her behaviours. She did, however, end up leaving the store to go to another job that she felt was a better fit for her overall; and that was the best thing for her and the store.

No matter what you believe, look to the numbers and statistics to prove it.

Simple Way to Increase the Average Sale

One easy way to bump up your average sale is to have your cashiers pick one product they really like in the store, and then have them work to add it on to each sale at the cash register. Because they like the product, it will be easier for them to sell. Any extra products you can add onto the original purchase will increase your average sale and improves your bottom line profit margin. Awesome!

Sometimes You Want to Go Where Everybody Knows Your Name

It pleases me a lot when I walk into my favourite coffee shop, and they remember who I am, which drink I like, and how I like it made. It makes me feel like they care; and because of that feeling, I go out of my way to go back there, rather than going to another coffee shop. On top of that, when they suggest I try something new on the menu, I am more likely to do it, because I trust that they have my best interest at heart, and they know what I really like. Trust and value. It all comes back to that. This is the experience you are going for in the Big Show.

When you take the time to get to know your customers - in particular your top 20% - simply because you want to know them better, it shows you care about them. When someone shows they truly care, it builds trust. When you have that, you have the basis of a great relationship. Based on that relationship, and knowing what the person values, you can make better suggestions about the products you have to offer, that will truly help them. Again, coming from a place of caring, you are not selling them something for the sake of selling them something. You are selling them a product, because you know it will help to make their life better in a way that's important to them. That's great customer service. That kind of great customer service will keep them coming back to you every time.

Pricing

I am completely an impulse buyer. If I find something I think is neat, and the price is right, I will buy it. The key is the pricing. Or more specifically, making sure the product has a price displayed. I have to know how much it is before I make the decision on its value for me. If I can't find the price, I put it back down and walk away, no matter how cool the item might be.

Pricing is part and parcel of the Big Show experience. Having a well-priced store will allow you to take advantage of those impulse buyers, and create a better experience for your customers over all. When your store is well priced, your customers are able to make more informed decisions about their purchases.

It will also help your sales team. Rather than running around trying to find the price of a product, they can spend more time with the customer, really finding out how they can meet their needs.

The bottom line is, a well-priced store creates an overall better environment for your customers, and that will lead to better sales for your business.

The Power of a Child

Never underestimate the power of a child when it comes to the buying decision of a parent. Children are large influencers in their own way. "Mom, can we get…," "Please Dad, you know I really need it…," "Please, please, please I will be good and you will never have to buy my anything ever, ever again." These are just some of the phrases every parent hears, that slowly and surely whittle away at the most heroic person's resolve, until they finally can't take it anymore, and give in just to save their own sanity.

There are also those children who will save their allowance forever to purchase what they want. The determination shown by some children is completely admirable.

And in truth, the way you treat a person's child or children will have a great bearing on how that person sees you. When my children were treated well by a sales person, I liked the sales person better, and I would rate my experience in the store higher. If my children were treated with indifference, or poorly, I was much less likely to buy, and way less likely to return to that store again.

So remember, treat the children well.

Be Our Guest

Disney understands exactly what is means to create the Big Show. Theirs is an experience like no other from start to finish and it all starts with the mindset of the company and the cast members.

I had the opportunity to listen to a speaker from Disney explain why they refer to their customers as guests. They recognize that guests are treated with reverence. When you invite guests into your home, you act differently, and you treat them differently. First of all, you probably clean up so everything is neat and tidy for their arrival. Then you might plan how you'll entertain them during their visit. When they arrive, you welcome them into your house, and probably give them a little tour, so they know where everything is. You'd offer them a drink, and maybe a seat to make them comfortable, and give them your full attention. When they leave, you thank them for coming over, and tell them you hope that you can get together again soon. In short, you go the distance to make them feel special, because they are your guests. That one word creates a mindset that sets up the experience.

In the Big Show, that's exactly the way a person should be treated when they walk through the doors of your store. They should be made to feel special and welcome, that they are the centre of your attention, and that you will do whatever it takes to make them comfortable and happy, so they'll want to come back again.

Sales Celebration

When you celebrate and reward great sales, your team will focus on creating more great sales. It really is a fantastic circle. You *will* get what you focus on. So with that in mind, why not set up a board in your staff room to share those great sales each day?

A sample board would include writing the name of the person who had the:

- Highest Daily Sales
- Highest Average Sale
- Highest Customer Count
- Highest Sales per Hour
- Highest Cumulative Sales for the Month
- Best Customer Compliment

Once it's set up, it won't be long before your team starts checking it every day. They will be excited and proud when their name holds the highest ranking.

Develop Vendor Relationships

As important as it is for you to get to know your staff and your customers, it's equally as important for you to get to know your vendors and the people who deliver your supplies. They really are an integral part of your company, and part of your Big Show. They have the ability to praise you to potential customers...or recommend that they go elsewhere. They can give you advice about what they see working in other stores that you might be able to adapt into your own store. They will have ideas that you might be able to use to create better systems. It all starts with building that relationship.

These people also work directly with your staff members on a completely different level than you do with them. You'd be surprised what you'll learn when you take the time to ask your vendors for feedback on your staff and your store.

Understand that I am not talking about a spy network to play Big Brother with your staff. What I am saying is that these people can give you a different perspective to help you initiate positive change. This has to come from a place of caring and with the intention that you want to do the best you can for your team, your customers, your store, and for the people who help you supply it.

Make people happy in every area of your business and your business will be happy.

Consumer Trends

In any retail business, you need to know the trends and seasons that affect the traffic flow coming into your store. By understanding that flow, you can adjust your staffing levels, product levels and varieties, your advertising and marketing plans, and so on.

A few examples that will affect your flow are:

- School breaks
- Holidays and long weekends
- Summer
- Christmas
- Release dates of government cheques
- Sporting events, like the Super Bowl or Stanley Cup playoffs

Planning for these will help you be fully prepared for the needs of your customers when they want something and your business.

Make a Day of it!

Remember, the Big Show always includes fun! Be creative. Subscribe to a calendar that lists all the crazy national or international days that are celebrated out there. Infuse some fun into your store, and use it. Who wouldn't enjoy Talk Like a Pirate Day? There's also Spaghetti Day, Hypnotism Day, National Tempura Day, Bubble Bath Day…seriously, there is a day for just about anything.

Have fun with it as you get your staff and customers involved!

Wage Control

Wages are one of the most controllable costs in your store. It's also an area that requires a fine balance. Adding people to an understaffed sales floor will help to increase sales, yet there is a point at which adding more sales people to your floor will do nothing to increase your sales. When there are too many sales people in your store and not enough customers, you are only wasting money by having them there. You have to find the balance that works for your particular business or location. The best way to do it is to analyze your historical data on your traffic flow, consider how many people one person can help in an hour, and then create your schedule from there.

For example, if you sell electronics, your sales person might spend the full hour with a customer, giving them the education they need to make the appropriate purchase. If your historical data shows you have an average of four customers in that particular hour, then you will need four sales people on hand to assist them. Having five people scheduled is just a waste of wages, since there will likely be no additional customers to help.

That all being said, you also have to realize that there will be anomalies in this planning, and you will have to adjust to it as necessary. Perhaps it's a particularly stormy day, and people just aren't coming out to shop. There is no point in keeping all of your staff on hand. If you send home two out of the four people who are working, you will accomplish two things. First and foremost, you will save on your wages. There's no point in paying someone to do nothing. That directly takes away from your bottom-line profit. You're also giving the other two people remaining the opportunity to make better sales. When there's less competition to reach the customer, each sales person has the ability to be more successful.

Naturally, you'll want to keep your best sales people on the floor, to be the most effective for your customers. Always remember that, when you make the decision to send someone home. Your poorest performers should be the first ones to leave.

Conversely, if for some reason you find there are more customers than your scheduled staff can handle, you can always call someone in to help with the rush.

It does take a little while to get a full handle on the balance you need to create. Just like anything in business, you must **analyze, adjust, and reset** as necessary. When it comes to retail scheduling and the balance of wages, it really is a never-ending process.

Rhyme and Reason When You're Down

The key is not to prioritize what's on your schedule, but to schedule your priorities. ~ Stephen Covey

If you're not meeting your sales goals, you will need to take the time to analyze where the issues lie. In retail, there are so many things that can affect the sales in the store. Stock levels, the store lay-out, product variety, marketing initiatives, staff scheduling, conversion rates…the list is nearly endless.

It's possible that there might be only one area in your store that's suffering; and if you improve that area, you will then solve the problem and increase your sales. More than likely though, there will be several areas that need improvement; and you'll need to decide which one of these areas will be the most effective for you to tackle, in order to turn your sales around and make up lost ground.

Let's pretend that we are a clothing store that is under the goal set for the month by $10K. The categories of Pants, Shirts, Shoes and Accessories are all down. Pants make up 10% of the overall sales, Shirts 30%, Shoes 15%, and Accessories 5%. It makes sense then, to focus on improving the sales in Shirts category, since it will have the biggest impact on the overall sales. This is not to say that the other categories get completely ignored. There just has to be reason applied to the focus of the energies used to promote the change.

When you are focusing on improving, work on one area at a time. Once it's under control, move to the next area, then the next, and so on. Trying to change too much at once will be ineffective and a waste of valuable resources (time, money, staff morale).

Once you have control, assess, analyze, and re-approach. The Big Show requires it.

Benefit From Your Competition

Your competition could be your best asset for increased growth,
ideas, and team leadership.

Know Your Competition

As a district manager, I had a store in an isolated area, but an area that had several options when it came to pet supplies. One of these options was a store the townspeople (fondly) referred to as "Stinky's." The nickname was apparently appropriate.

My supervisor asked me if I had gone into the store to check out what our competition was doing. While I had checked out other stores, I hadn't gone into that one because, in my mind, there was no competition from a store that was so obviously awful.

It was pointed out to me that if they were still open, they still had customers. And if they still had customers, they were doing something right, and I could probably learn something from it, especially since there were other things that were so obviously not working.

Well. Wasn't that a kicker?

I'm not saying copy everything your competition does. That will just make you second best. Recognize there are things they do well, and maybe better than you. The thing is to know it. Study it. Learn from it. Adapt it or discard it. But most of all, respect it.

Get Focused

Whether you think you can or whether you think you can't, you're right. ~ Henry Ford

Whatever you choose to focus on, you will get.

Why not make it positive?

Who is Your Competition?

The most obvious answer to the question is the businesses that offer the same types of products you have. On the surface, this is true, but it's more than that. It doesn't matter what kind of business you have, there are only a certain number of consumer dollars available out there to spend. There are a lot of things for a consumer to spend it on: books, clothes, computers, televisions, trips, sports, music, vehicles, and so much more. The question then becomes, why should the consumer take their hard earned money and shop with you to buy what you have to offer?

The Big Show creates the desire for what you have. To flame that desire, focus on the things that make your store and your products unique. Hire the best people and make the customer experience in your store second to none. Only then, the consumers just might choose to come to you.

Motivate for Accountability

The best way to motivate your team is teaching them how they have power and impact on your business success.

Balance and Equality

In any retail organization, one of the biggest challenges for the leader is balancing the operational tasks with the sales goals. When the Big Show is your goal, that balance is a must. The most efficient way to create balance is to assign tasks to each of your staff members, with the expectation that they complete the tasks in between helping customers.

What generally happens is the person who does the operational tasks the best and most efficiently, often gets saddled with almost all of them. This can be very frustrating because, in essence, they're getting punished for doing a good job by having more work assigned to them, while other team members do little to operationally help out.

It kind of reminds me of a quote from George Orwell's *Animal Farm*, **"All animals are equal, but some animals are more equal than others."** In order to run your store well, there has to be balance for everyone; but the reality is that everyone isn't built equally. Not all of them can handle the challenge of completing larger tasks and sales at the same time. It comes down to knowing your team. You have to get to know the abilities of each person. For those who don't handle the multitasking well, give them shorter, more easily accomplished tasks. You also might want to consider keeping them in an area where you can easily see them, and direct them to your customers as necessary. The ones that can handle more complicated tasks let them run with it. Remember to let them know why they are being assigned to it. Positively reinforcing your "go-to" guy or gal is a good thing all around.

Making sure that everyone is assigned a task to do during his or her shift will help to keep the store looking great, and create better equality for all.

Delegation

Learning to delegate is one of the most important skills a leader can have in their toolbox. When you become a leader you gain more responsibility than one person can deal with. In the Big Show, you have a lot going on. If you don't delegate you won't get everything done. Delegating should be easy, right? Just tell someone what to do and they get it done. How hard is that?

Before you became a leader, you likely came out of situation where you had contributed to the support of other leaders, which is why you were promoted in the first place. You are an expert in getting things done quickly and efficiently. Now part of your job will be to watch over less experienced team members and that's going to liven things up. You are probably more capable of doing the individual work than those who report to you. They have less experience, and that means their solutions might not be well designed, and because of that they will take more time to implement.

If you, as a leader, can solve a problem or complete a task in two days, where it will take someone else five days, you will probably just do it yourself. It makes perfect sense, because you will get a better solution faster. But what if you are in charge of 5 people? What about 30 people? How about 100 people? At some point the math doesn't work. You can't work hard or fast enough to complete the work of all those people under you. You can do one task better or faster, but not all of them.

It's important to hand off responsibility to those "less capable" for two main reasons. First, you don't have time to do everything. You will never be able to complete all of your staff's duties, as well as all of the tasks and roles of a leader.

Second, if you never hand off responsibility to members of your team, they will never grow. Why are you, as their leader, able to get all these things done so well and so quickly? You have the experience under your belt. You've done it before, so you are efficient at it. But remember, you have that experience and efficiency because someone else trusted you to do it. It may take your team member 5 days to complete the task, but next time, it will take them 4, and then 3, and then who knows? They could become better at it than you. Scary thought? Not at all! If they're able to step in and fill your shoes, you can move on to bigger and better things, like delegating to 200, or even 700 team members. Imagine that; taking the Show to the next level!

The key to delegation is giving people the opportunity to grow and that also means the opportunity to fail. Two sides of the same coin, really. Succeeding or failing is still an opportunity to learn. Growing the skills of your team will make you successful as a leader. Your team will be able to take on higher and tougher goals, and solve them more quickly. Leaders who do all the work on their own won't grow, and are writing their own prescription for failure. Delegation is part of the success that helps you to create the wonder in the Big Show.

Your Game, Your Rules

What you cannot enforce / Do not command. ~ Sophocles

I had an employee who was continually late. The rule in my store was that if you let me know at least 15 minutes prior to your shift that you would be late, you didn't get documented for the infringement. If there was no notification, you were documented, and on your third documentation, you were terminated.

After several calls notifying me of tardiness, I sat the employee down, and we had a chat about this unacceptable behaviour. I learned that he had to take the bus to work every day, and the times the bus ran by his stop didn't fit well with the times he was scheduled to work. He could either be an hour early or 15 minutes late.

Now personally, I would have opted to be an hour early, but I do realize everyone is not like me. Understanding this, I adjusted his shift to start 30 minutes later. A win-win situation all around, I thought, and he agreed.

So what happened?

The employee, having an extra 30 minutes, decided to take a later bus, and was late. He got terminated.

Sometimes you have to realize that no matter what you do, some people aren't motivated to work in your environment. That's okay. It just means they're meant to be somewhere else. Don't hang onto the people who don't want to play the game your way. And stick to your guns.

Mindset

Ability is what you're capable of doing. Motivation determines what you do. Attitude determines how well you do it. ~ Lou Holtz

'Nuf said.

Can I Quote That?

Quotes can motivate, inspire, reach us emotionally, and educate. In your staffroom, create an area where you share a quote of the day. Get your team involved, and have them share a quote they like.

As long as it's clean, anything goes.

Educate, Motivate, and Inspire

Like it or not part of your job as a leader is to motivate and inspire. Running the Big Show means you have to make sure your team is "on" all the time. That means you have to be on all the time too. Sometimes you're a boss, sometimes a parent, and sometimes a mentor. At all times, you have the unique opportunity to make the people around you greater through your actions, words, and counsel. It's part of how you create the sparkle in the centre ring. Take it seriously. Only you can make the choice to be the best you can be. Educate yourself by reading books to develop that motivational side of you.

Here are 5 books to get you started:

1. *Tuesdays With Morrie* by Mitch Albom: It will teach you how to live your life fully.

2. *Oh, the Places You'll Go* by Dr. Seuss: Yup, I know it's a children's book, but the message is clear. And let's face it, Dr. Seuss is fun! And if you can't have fun, what's the point of it all?

3. *Fish! A Proven Way to Boost Morale and Improve Results* by Stephen C. Lundin, Harry Paul, John Christensen and Kevin Blanchford: It's fun and it'll make you want you and your team to be "World Famous" too (it's in the book).

4. *Who Will Cry for You When You Die* by Robin Sharma: This book gives some great pointers to develop and centre yourself. A calmer and stronger you will make a calmer and stronger leader for everyone around you.

5. *Start With WHY* by Simon Sinek: It will challenge you to define your true purpose as a leader not just in business, but also in life.

Making it Better

The biggest room in the world is the room for improvement.
~Anonymous

Do one thing today to make yourself a better leader, improve the look of your store, or create a better system. Take one step closer to the Big Show, no matter how big or small it is.

When you are always looking to get better and be better, what you offer will never be stale. That's very valuable.

Track Your Success

Create a file to record your successes as a leader. In here, you can track each time you exceed your sales targets, file any customer compliments about you, your employees or your store, record notes on the development and promotion of your employees, list any courses you have completed or books you've read to make you a better leader, and so on.

When it comes time for an annual review, or perhaps time to request a performance review, it will be easier to articulate why you deserve a raise because you have document proof of your success and contribution.

It's also a great way to pat yourself on the back and celebrate your wins as a retail leader.

All Eyes on You

If there is such a thing as good leadership, it is to give a good example. ~ Ingvar Kamprad

Always remember, your team watches you at all times. You are the leader of the Show they star in every day. What you do makes a difference. They notice what you wear, and if it meets the set standards, whether or not you're punctual, who you talk to and for how long, how you interact with the team, and so much more. You are their leader and they look to you for clues on behaviour and what's acceptable. They know when you're just talking the talk.

In good conscience, you cannot hold your team accountable for things you don't follow through on yourself. You completely ruin your credibility when you follow the "do as I say, not as I do" theory.

You also can't hold one person accountable for a certain set of behaviours, and not make it the same for everyone else. That shows favouritism, which will shake the foundations of the team and the motivation in the store.

Lead by example, follow the rules, uphold the rules equally, and gain the credibility and respect of those around you.

A Clear Understanding

Management is efficiency in climbing the ladder of success; leadership determines whether the ladder is leaning against the right wall. ~ Stephen R. Covey

I had a manager who was very frustrated that his staff weren't fronting and facing the store - neatly squaring all the products on the shelves with the English label out - to his liking. He complained that when he told them to fix a section, it pretty much looked the same as it had before.

The way I see it, there are two possibilities in this type of situation: 1) the staff members were wilfully ignoring, or not completing the set of behaviours he had outlined, which would indicate huge problems in his management skills over all, or 2) they didn't understand how to do the task in the first place.

As you may have guessed, the problem was the latter. When he took one employee and asked her to show him how to front and face a section, it was clear she had very little understanding of what she was actually supposed to do. Fifteen minutes of training later, the issue was solved, permanently. He had to repeat the process with his entire team, and from there forward, he could be sure everyone had a full understanding of what was required. *Now*, he had the full right to be upset and hold them accountable for not doing the task properly, if they failed to do so.

The lesson, before becoming upset about an issue in your store with your staff members, make sure they have a clear understanding of what it is you want in the first place.

Very few people go to work to intentionally do a bad job. All too often, what they end up with is really bad training, and, therefore, they lack the ability to do what's required of them, to their full potential.

Creating Worth

The art of choosing men is not nearly so difficult as the art of enabling those one has chosen to attain their full worth. ~ Napoleon Bonaparte

Do one thing today that will develop the skills of someone on your team.

Follow Up

Any time you set an assignment, or coach your staff on adjusting their behaviours, you need to set a deadline for completion. This will give them a clear understanding of when they're expected to complete what you have outlined.

On top of that, you also need to set follow-up dates, to make sure your employees are able to complete what you've asked them to do, within the timeline you've given.

Whether it's for a large assignment, like re-pricing a full section, or maybe it's adjusting a person's selling behaviours on your sales floor, setting follow-up dates will allow you to do three things. First, it shows you actually care about the progress the person is making, which will go a long way to creating a feeling of being valued.

Second, it allows you the opportunity to give them help if they require it, and/or adjust the final deadline if necessary. Again, it shows you care and have compassion for the person, and it sets the person up for success, even if the deadline has to be adjusted. Most often, it's the learning experience for your staff member that's most important, not the deadline.

Finally, it gives you the opportunity to provide encouragement and positive reinforcement, and that is always a good thing. We are human, after all.

Follow-up is much more than just making sure the task gets done. It shows you're a leader who actually cares about the success of your store and your team, and that you're willing to commit yourself to helping them achieve it.

Get to Their Why

Knowing that we're a part of a larger purpose often gives a greater sense of satisfaction. It's being part of that greater good. This is something you should take to heart with your team. When people understand why they've been given a certain task, and how completing that task will help the overall scheme of things, they will often be much more willing to do what needs to be done.

A staff member might be annoyed when you hand them a broom and a mop, and tell them to go clean the floors. However, if you let that same staff member know that you're completing the larger job of fully cleaning up your store, and that each member of the team is being assigned a task to help out with doing that, they'll (hopefully) be more understanding about what you're asking them to do. You could even take it a step further, and explain how cleaning the store will create a better environment for the staff and the customers; and that might give even more value to the job.

Most people want to see the bigger picture, but often can't do it on their own. When you back them away far enough to see the entirety, you give them clarity. When they understand their actions will have an impact on a larger level, and they can see how they are a part of making it better, they'll be more motivated to do what you need them to do. Whether it's cleaning up, or seeing how each person impacts the success of the store through their sales and customer service, having the ability to see the big picture creates more satisfaction for the job over all. They can understand how they add to the experience that goes into orchestrating the Big Show.

Just Be

Take time to be alone, and just be.

Often in those moments of quiet, we find our greatest ideas and solutions to our problems. Create the space for the thoughts to come.

The Top 10 Wish List

You need to be aware of what others are doing, applaud their efforts, acknowledge their successes, and encourage them in their pursuits. When we all help one another, everybody wins. ~ Jim Stovall

I had a supervisor who came to me and said she would like to do something at our next staff meeting, that a former employer did for her. She wanted to give our team the opportunity to write down 10 things they wished they had for the store.

Now, I really want to say to you that I embraced the idea, especially since she was stepping up and actively looking for new ways to make the store a better place. But no, instead, I said that I thought it was a dumb idea, because they would probably ask for stupid things, like a slurpee machine for the staffroom. Yup. Complete and total honesty...I really sucked as a leader on that day. However, to somewhat redeem myself, I would like to say that when I went home that night, I couldn't get her idea out of my head. And the more I thought about it, the more I thought that she really was onto something with it. So what if they asked for a slurpee machine? At least I would know they were motivated by slurpees, and it could be a great reward for them when they did something that should be celebrated. I apologized to her the next day, and told her it really was a great idea, and to go for it.

When I got the top 10 wish lists back from the staff members, I was completely shocked. It was a second lesson for me. What they wished for were plain, simple things, like an extra broom and mop, so they could complete their closing tasks more quickly and efficiently. They asked for tools to make them more effective at their jobs. It was a humbling experience, and an enlightening one. My team really wanted to do their best, and I never knew we weren't meeting their needs, until that moment.

Honour that wonderful supervisor who taught me some invaluable lessons. Try out the top 10 wish list on your staff. It might be just as

---

enlightening for you as it was for me, and help you to create a new inspiration for your Big Show.

Squeeze a Pig

On days when things weren't quite going my way, I would take a minute to pick up a pink plush pig toy we had in the store, and squeeze it. It made the most hilarious grunting noise that never failed to make me smile and lighten my mood.

What do you have that does the same thing for you? Look for your pink pig.

10 Pennies and a Nickel

A coach is someone who can give correction without causing resentment. ~ John Wooden

The Big Show experience requires a lot of coaching on your part. If you find your staff members become angry or defensive when you deliver corrective coaching, then you may need to operate on the 10 pennies and a nickel rule of guidance. The pennies are for compliments and encouragement. The nickel is for delivering feedback on corrective behaviours. Of course, with Canada's elimination of the penny, you can use whatever coins or objects you wish to represent the compliments and corrective side of your coaching. The idea is to focus on being more positive and encouraging. As a leader, you will always have to deliver some form of correction if you're doing your job properly. Your staff members have to learn what it is that they need to do, and what is expected of them. It doesn't come magically; it comes with coaching and training. People are more likely to gracefully accept correction when it's not the only thing they hear.

Keep the coins in your pocket, and transfer a penny to a different pocket each time you pay a compliment or give encouragement. The nickel transfers when you deliver a correction. Only once all the pennies are transferred, can you start again with the ability to deliver another correction. If you didn't use the nickel, then give yourself a pat on the back, and keep going with the compliments. If you did use the nickel, make sure you watch for the changed behaviour; and when it happens, be sure to reinforce it with encouragement.

Everyone wants to feel like they're doing a good job. And when their good work is noticed, they'll be more likely to keep focusing on the good work. The reinforcement needs to come from you.

The Best Intentions

You know failure isn't failure, if a lesson from it's learned. ~ Kent Blazy and Garth Brooks

I had a young gentleman on my team whom I thought was quite brilliant. He was personable and charming, and I knew he could be a fantastic salesperson. It was his first sales job, so I decided I was going to help him as much as I could. Each hour, I would go over his sales, giving him pointers on making his presentation better. I coached on opening the sale, how to add on, how to close, anything I thought could help. Yes! He was getting everything he needed to succeed.

Three months later, he quit. It was only during a conversation with a supervisor, that I found out he quit because he thought I didn't like him. I was floored. I did what I had done because I liked him so much. My best intention had backfired in the worst kind of way.

I realize now that I had made three very key mistakes. The first was not letting him know what I was doing in the first place. Had I sat him down, shared my plan, and told him that I thought he was amazing, and had such wonderful potential, he might have viewed my coaching in a completely different way. Perhaps he would have had a clear understanding of my intention.

The second mistake was a lack of positive support. Instead of celebrating his wins, I looked for ways to continue to help him with his shortcomings. The message I sent was that nothing he could do was good enough. Each time I coached, he would change his behaviour and get better, but then I would come up with something else he needed to improve. That is flat out discouraging on any level.

Finally, my third mistake was not setting up time for us to meet together, off the sales floor, so he could give me feedback about my coaching. Even with the other two mistakes in place, it's possible that a quick meeting with him to go over my coaching style could have resolved the problems that were building. Feedback is just as important for the coach, as it is for the person being coached. No matter how good a coach may be, it doesn't always mean their style is well matched to coach the person who needs the help. With feedback, I could have adapted my coaching to suit his needs better, or I could have found another coach on my team that worked more effectively with his particular needs and communication style.

One thing I have learned is that we all make mistakes, some bigger and more impactful than others. The key is to learn from them and grow. I hope sharing this particular set of mistakes will help you learn the same lesson in a much kinder way.

Have Fun

What's the point in creating the Big Show if you don't enjoy it? You have to be able to create your own fun in your job, because if you don't love what you're doing, why are you doing it?

One leader I know would serenade his staff with random songs over the intercom before the store opened. He was completely tone deaf. Another did happy dances in the middle of the store with her staff or customers, because it made her feel good; and inevitably, it would always make them smile. And yet another spent a day answering his staff with a ping-pong ball. One side of the ball had a happy face, and the other side, a sad face. When a staff member asked to go on their scheduled break, he would hold up the smiley face. A staff member asking to go home early might get the sad face. It highly amused him, and the staff had a good time with it too.

Your own brand of fun will be uniquely yours; but guaranteed, it will brighten your day, and show your staff, and perhaps your customers, your sense of humour. That's all part of the Big Show, Baby!

Accountability

Your store's ability to run efficiently and effectively is directly related to the measure of accountability you have for your staff. The higher the accountability level, the better the team is at doing their jobs. The better the team is at doing their jobs, the better your store will perform. The better the performance, the better the Show.

People operate better in a structured system, when they have a very clear view of their responsibilities. When accountability is not in place, the outline of those duties and behaviours becomes fuzzy. How can a person function appropriately when he or she is unsure of the parameters of their position? Every person needs to know what he or she has to do when they are in the spotlight.

Accountability does more than apply corrective behaviours or discipline. It levels the playing field for everyone involved. When you hold accountability for your team equally across the board, everyone will know exactly what the consequence will be if they don't act in the way they are supposed to act. And they will know it will be the same for everyone, every time. This creates equality as everyone is treated exactly the same way, showing you don't have favourites, and cutting down on potential staff resentment. In short, it's fair. It also creates respect for you as a leader, because you treat people equally, and you are giving them a structure that makes sense. It creates an environment that people will want to work in.

When you lack accountability, you are basically giving your team free reign to do whatever they like. Essentially, you are saying, "It would be really nice if you showed up to work on time, but if you don't, oh well. I'm not going to do anything about it anyway." That's not management or leadership. It's the complete lack of it. Not holding accountability is only making *you* feel better. You are limiting the potential of your team by not giving them the feedback - and guidelines - they need to succeed. You are holding them back from excelling in the best way they can. You are holding back the Big Show. Yes, disciplining a staff member is never fun. However, once you have a good accountability level in your store, you will find you have to do it less and less often. And you'll probably find that with greater accountability, your team is much happier working together as each member is taking accountability for his or her own work.

Bring a Solution

Everybody needs to vent occasionally about his or her job. That's human nature. Your job as the leader of the Big Show is to encourage your team to make it an effective endeavour. If they are going to vent, they should vent to a person who can help them with the situation. Venting to another staff member is only creating a negative environment. That works against the magic you are working to create. Approaching one of the leaders on the team gives them the opportunity to assist in making a change that will be helpful for the whole team. Most likely, if one person is upset about an issue in the store, there are more people who feel the same way, but aren't voicing their concerns.

Impress upon your team that they need to be proactive in the situation. When they talk about an issue, it would be more effective to come with a possible solution or solutions. As a leader, you never know when your team will come up with a more effective way of getting things done in the store. Feedback is always a good thing, especially when it comes from the people directly involved. When you are working toward creating an amazing experience for everyone involved, feedback is a true gift for you and for them. People want to know they have a voice. Full consideration needs to be given to their ideas; and if it's possible, they should be put into place. It's also okay not to use their ideas. A face-to-face meeting gives you the opportunity to discuss why their solution doesn't actually work within the bigger picture. That might give them better clarity for the situation. Either way, allowing your team to have their ideas heard will give them a greater sense of satisfaction overall. Think back to the chapter on the Top 10 Wish List. This allowed my team to provide great feedback and solutions as to what would make our store more effective. Each individual member had input into their needs, some of which I was able to implement. True changes only come about if you allow your team to be part of the solution. Stop relying on just yourself to have all the answers; your team is most likely full of them. Create an environment where sharing solutions is encouraged. Create the environment that promotes the Big Show.

It's Always Been That Way

Just because something has always been done a particular way in your store, doesn't mean it's the best, right, or most efficient way of doing it. Take a step back and evaluate some of your systems and practices. Is there a way to make it better?

Always looking to get better is exactly what goes into perfect the Big Show.

Take Action

Remember, a position doesn't make a leader, but a leader can make the position. ~ John C. Maxwell, *The 360° Leader*

It's your actions that make you a leader, not your title. Use your integrity, stay true to your beliefs, and people will notice.

Just Ask

When I was younger, going shopping with my dad was a mortifying experience. It didn't matter what store we went to, my dad would always ask for a deal. In my whiney teenager voice, I'd admonish him with a two syllable "Daa-aaaad," punctuated with a heavy sigh and scathing eye roll, while I looked around to see if anybody was watching the "greatest embarrassment on earth" take place.

"What?" he would say. "The worst they can do is say no."

In my adult years, I finally got it. People who ask for what they want, more often than not, get it. The people that want it and don't ask sit on the sidelines, living on empty wishes and dreams.

The majority of the time, my dad got the things he asked for, and it made him feel good.

So, ask for the promotion. Ask for the upgrade to first class on your next flight. Ask for the help you need. Whatever it is, just ask. You just might get exactly what you're asking for.

Value vs. Resistance

If you've taken any kind of sales course, you've probably learned that when you can increase the value of the product in your customer's eyes, you will reduce their resistance to the price. Makes sense, right? If I feel the product is good, and can place value on how it will make my life easier, and make me look better, feel better, or whatever, I can justify spending money on it.

I believe this principle can also be applied to other areas of your personal and professional life. Think about it. We all have our own personal values and belief systems. The more we believe in something, the more value we can create for it in our lives, whatever "it" may be.

Let's say you really want to lose weight. The more you can justify how losing that weight will affect your life, the more likely you are to do it. Maybe losing weight will make you feel better about yourself. It will get you out more, make you healthier, help you to enjoy life more, and maybe even find the person of your dreams. The more the outcome means to you, the more likely you will be to do whatever it is you're thinking about.

On a professional level, you can manage change by using the same principles of value vs. resistance. When change happens, you will inevitably meet with resistance. People don't like change. It's new and it's scary. Change pushes people into a zone where they aren't comfortable, where they might not be able to predict the outcome of this new situation. But if you can justify and personalize how that change is going to make their work life better, or easier, or more fun, the more likely they are going to be to accept that change. The more you connect with their values and what's important to them, the more you're going to have their buy-in for the change. It will be a smoother process in the long run, and it's much more likely to be successful.

Are You Bored?

When a mature and able manager feels bored, he should seriously consider changing jobs, changing companies - or simply retiring. It is not fair to anyone for half a leader to hold a full-time leadership job. ~ James L. Hayes

You can't create the Big Show that way. Pretty good food for thought. Just sayin'.

And to Quote

There's something about how a poignant quote can get your point across in a way that no other communication medium can. If you're looking for great quotes to share, motivate, or inspire your team, you can find a plethora with just a few clicks of your keyboard and mouse. There are so many sites on the Internet that can help with inspiration, motivation, leadership, management, spirituality, and so on.

Here are a few that have helped me find the quote I need:

- Brainyquote.com
- Leadershipnow.com
- Quotegarden.com
- Thinkexist.com
- Staymotivated.info

Simply understand your purpose for needing a quote and the message you're trying to convey and you'll find one that supports your needs.

The 1% Rule

You know the key to rocking it in the Big Show is to strive for continuous improvement. It doesn't have to be monumental leaps to greatness. Expecting that from yourself is overwhelming. Instead, it's about taking baby steps to greatness. Can you make yourself 1% better at something today? That's not a hard task. It could be as simple as filing some of the papers on your desk. A few minutes and you're done.

Could you make yourself 1% better tomorrow? Sure. No problem. Now that the papers are filed, you could clean up the scattered pens and pencils, and put them in a holder. Maybe add the scissors, so you know where they are. Easy. You could even get crazy and put the paperclips in a holder too.

What if you did it again the next day? And the next? What if you got your management team to do the same thing? That would mean your store would be 365% better at the end of the year. That's a pretty big change. And it's all done with little steps.

Take a moment and think: what's your first 1% going to be?

The Blame Game

It starts as little kids. "It was Jimmy's fault. He was the one that told me to…" It then continues as we grow into adults. "Nancy didn't explain what I had to do to complete the project properly. I didn't really understand that I had to…" In reality, they are simply excuses we make for ourselves, when we don't want to truly own up to the choices we have made. As a child, we made the choice to follow Jimmy down the path he was leading, even though we knew it was wrong. After all, Jimmy didn't actually drag us there, and force us to do whatever it was, under pain of death. And as an adult, we made the choice not to ask Nancy to clarify, or to give further information, so we could have appropriately completed what was asked. Nancy was just simply the excuse we used to cover our own poor behaviour.

Now it's time to hold up the mirror. Where are you putting blame on other people for the choices you have, in actuality, made for yourself? How can you change those behaviours to become better at being accountably you?

Growth can only come when you recognize that you have some areas that need improvement. We are human after all and we are not infallible. We all have room to grow. Where you start, starts with you.

Monitor and Make a Difference

Remember, it's too late to change anything when you reach the end of the day. When you monitor your progress throughout the day, you have the opportunity to make a difference. And making a difference is what truly great leaders are all about.

Success Breeds Happiness

When people are successful at what they do, they're much happier. Your team needs to know how they can contribute and how their contribution makes a difference over all.

What can you do to create success for someone on your team today?

Removing the "Overwhelm"

Sometimes we get busy versus being productive, because we're so overwhelmed we try to FEEL productive. ~ Robin Sharma

Running the Big Show takes a lot of work. There are a lot of moving parts and it isn't easy to keep everything running smoothly. Overwhelm often happens when we have so much going on that we don't even know where to start to make it better. When you're in that place, it's time to take a step back and evaluate your tasks, or your current course of action. There is a way through the chaos in front of you.

Try this exercise:

1. Get a package of sticky notes.
2. On each one, write down each of the tasks you need to accomplish.
3. From left to right, place them in order of importance. The best way to do that is to ask yourself which task will affect the most areas of importance. The one that will make the biggest impact goes first.
4. Under each task, with separate sticky notes, write down all the steps that need to be completed to fully finish the task. For example, clean the bathroom would have the steps of cleaning the walls, floor, mirror, toilet, sink, counter, refill paper towel, refill toilet paper, etc.
5. Assign dates for execution for each of the smaller tasks.
6. Remove the sticky note when each task is complete.

Now you have an action plan that will move you from overwhelmed to on your way!

Supporting Your Staff

The best way to see your staff thrive is by hiring the right people for the right role, then giving them the proper tools they need.

The Sales Interview

Hire character. Train skill. ~ *Peter Schutz*

The Big Show requires a certain kind of person. Not everyone fits the bill. In order to get the right person for the right position, you have to ask better questions. When you're hiring a sales person, make sure you ask sales-oriented questions. Whether it's evaluating how they might handle various situations with a customer, or learning their feeling about sales and sales goals, it will give you a good idea of where they stand on doing sales for a living.

One of my favourite things to do about half way through the interview is to ask a prospective candidate to sell me the pen I'm holding. This does a few things for you. First, you can see how well a person reacts on their feet. I have had some people stammer and work their way through, and other people who are able to present all the advantages and benefits of the pen easily. A customer is bound to ask something they are not fully trained to handle. It will give a good indicator of how flustered they might be in any given situation.

Secondly, it will tell you how a person might react when being put on the spot or under pressure. I've had a couple of candidates out rightly refuse to sell me the pen. Now, I can understand being nervous, or asking for a little time to think about it. I can't understand refusing to sell me something when applying for a sales job. The reality is, they are going to have to sell stuff every day. So, what here is the problem? It's a huge red flag. If they're going to refuse to answer a question in an interview, what will happen when they start working for you?

Finally, it tells you how they can sell. Some people naturally pick out features / benefits of a product and match them to your needs. That's the kind of person you want, because selling comes easily for them. But don't rule out candidates solely based on this one question. If you find a great personality fit for your store, hire them. You can teach them what they need to know to sell. That's why you have training in place. This scenario will also point out those candidates who might need a little extra coaching when they start out. Knowing it before they take the stage will help you get them ready for their time in the spotlight.

Hiring for Leader Positions

People are definitely a company's greatest asset. It doesn't make any difference whether the product is cars or cosmetics. A company is only as good as the people it keeps. ~ Mary Kay Ash

Hiring a leader for the Big Show is no easy feat. All too often, I've hired someone who seemed to be great in an interview and was a nightmare in the store. It took a lot of evaluating and re-evaluating the processes to get it right. The key, of course, is to find the person that best matches the values of the business and the team. That someone will have the same work ethic, integrity and drive that fits with you and your team. That sparkle that makes them the right fit to take their place in the centre ring.

Finding the right person starts with the ad you place. Just about anyone who has management experience will be able to fulfill the duties you need done within your business, but you are not looking for someone who can simply complete a task. That doesn't fit the Big Show ideal. You're looking for someone who enhances the team you have in place. When you place your ad, you need to focus on the qualities it takes to be successful within your team. Rather than focusing on the duties you need them to do, like cash reconciliation, supervision, and sales, focus on the ideals of someone who loves the challenge of coaching a team to success, who will find innovative and creative solutions by looking at angles the average manager doesn't even notice, and someone who believes that when a team works together, everyone benefits. Let's face it, almost anyone can meet the first criteria we laid out, but the second set is a very unique person indeed.

Now comes the interview process. I personally think a minimum of three interviews is necessary for any position, but especially leader positions of any type. Some companies will have even more interviews than that. You have to find the balance that's right for your company. One thing to keep in mind, the more important the position, the more difficult it should be to get the job, and the more in-depth the interview process. If you hire a leader or supervisor based on one interview in the food court, what does that really say about your company? It implies desperation, and you never want to be in that boat when you are looking to fill a position on your management team. You can't create magic from that kind of place.

I also believe the interviews should be done by two or three different people. This will give you a broader spectrum of impressions about the candidates. You could also opt for panel interviews, which you may find more efficient. Naturally, the person(s) you choose to assist you with the interview process need to understand the values of your team, and what will best suit it. The final decision, of course, will be yours to make.

Make sure you take notes during the interviews, and let the candidates know you will be doing so. Write down your thoughts and impressions about the answers. This will help you qualify the candidates more easily at the end, especially when you have different people interviewing the candidates.

I have given sample questions in each of the following interview sections to get you started on creating your own set of questions. The questions need to be unique to your business, and focus on the elements that make up a good candidate for you and your company. Everyone will have vastly different needs, depending on what you need to succeed.

First Interview

The first interview should be short and sweet. Basically, here you are weeding out the people who shouldn't be in the running. You're getting a feel for what they know about the company, how his or her personality might fit your team, and their general knowledge for management. This can be an interview that is completed over the phone, or you could train your cashiers to ask certain questions when the resume is handed in to them.

I also believe that if you are considering a person for the second stage of the interview process, you should hand the candidate off to another employee who is not on the management team, to give a store tour directly after their first interview. The person leading the tour should be chatty, and look to learn a little more about the person as they lead the tour. It's basically an informal part of the process that will let you know how the person reacts to your staff and the store when their guard is down. People react differently in more formal situations, versus a more relaxed one. You want to know that this person will treat everyone on your team with the respect they deserve, no matter what the position, and this is an effective way to check that, right at the start.

Expect this interview to last about 30 minutes (if the candidate is doing well, of course). If you come across a reason the person is not suitable for the position, end the interview quickly. Don't waste your time.

First Interview Sample Questions:

- Beyond the obvious (brands, products, etc), why do you want to work here?
- Tell me about your greatest success as a leader.
- How will this position help you achieve your goals?
- What type of people do you find challenging to work with? (Everyone has someone)
- What makes you laugh?
- What makes you angry?
- Tell me about a time where you helped someone succeed.
- What type of environment or culture suits you best?
- What other businesses have cultures that you admire?

These are all questions that will tell you about the values of the person you're interviewing. You will also want to check out any gaps in the resume, job jumping, reason for leaving the last position, and so on. This will tell you about their work history and potential work habits.

Ask for references and use them. You will be surprised at what a reference might say about the candidate. Make sure you check the references before proceeding to the next interviews. There is no point in continuing with the interview process if the references don't check out. Again, don't waste your time.

Second Interview

The second interview should be based on why the candidate should stay in the running for the job. Here, you're really looking at what makes the person fit with your team, how they thrive in the work environment, and if their skills will suit the position. Can they run the Show?

This is going to be much more in-depth, and will deal with more of the situational aspects of the job, and what they have done before. Wherever possible, you will want to use real situations you have encountered within your business, to see how the person would handle them. This will include customer complaints, staff situations, sales solutions, and so on.

You should expect this interview to last a minimum of an hour, and probably closer to two, since you will be getting a much more in-depth look into the person's experiences.

Second Interview Sample Questions

- Give the candidate a list of ten tasks that must be completed during the day, and ask them to assign an importance to each, with one being the most important. Then ask why they prioritized the tasks in the way they did. This will give good insight into how they might balance their daily tasks, and why certain ones will hold more significance. If you want to see how they delegate, you could follow up with a question of how they would get this done by the end of the shift.
- Address a real customer complaint situation.
- Create a scenario or give a real example of conflict between staff members, and ask how they would solve it.
- Pose three fictional staff members who need sales coaching in different areas. Ask how they would help each one to achieve success.
- Create a scenario where the actions of an employee should lead to a termination, and see if they opt to terminate or keep the employee. Find out why they made the decision.

- Looking at a real or fictional profit and loss statement, ask what areas they would address in order to increase the bottom line profit.
- How would you help to control theft?
- Tell me about the manager that had the greatest impact on your career, and why.
- Tell me why I should hire you instead of the other candidate who is equally qualified.

Third Interview

The third interview is the final decision making time. Here, you want to really zone in on why and how this person will grow your team and help it to reach new heights. As a business, you want to be getting better all the time, and this person needs to help you achieve that. How will they shine in the spotlight?

Again, I would expect this interview to last a minimum of an hour.

Third Interview Sample Questions

- Take the person onto your sales floor, and have them indicate what they would change in the store to make it better.
- Tell me about a time where you coached or mentored someone to a promotion or to greater success.
- Tell me about the worst leader you had, and why you consider them to be so.
- Learning from the experience above, what would you do differently as a leader here?
- Tell me about a time where you came up with an innovative solution to a problem.
- What attributes do you bring to the management team that will make it stronger?

Whatever interview questions you decide to use for any of your interviews, you need to make them standard for all your candidates, at all the stages. You cannot compare apples to apples if you are going to use a different selection process for each one. Standard interview questions are a must.

Supervisors Galore

Instead of waiting for a leader you can believe in, try this: Become a leader you can believe in. ~ Stan Slap

I once knew a manager who really understood how to create the Big Show. He had eight supervisors on his 40-person team. I thought he was insane, and I certainly didn't understand the Big Show concept, not even a little. Surely, having that many was both excessive and unnecessary.

Now, fast forward to Christmas of that year, when I had only two other supervisors to manage with me, and we had to survive the holiday season. Who bailed my butt out? You guessed it.

That manager had it worked out. By having many more supervisors than he needed, he never got stuck when someone called in sick, went on vacation, or quit. He made sure he was never behind the eight ball.

His supervisors had to be trained in all areas of his store, so they could direct and lead, or take over any section or position whenever he needed it. They had to be more than proficient in operations, sales, product knowledge, and leadership. He laid down the groundwork to create a strong team.

More importantly, becoming a supervisor in his store was a great achievement. It was something to truly be celebrated, because in order to be a supervisor, you had to prove you could make his team better. And every single employee in the store knew that was the criteria for it. He had created the desire to achieve. He had created exactly what he needed for the Big Show.

It's a smart lesson to learn.

Psst....Pass It On

The telephone game is a popular way to show just how badly a message is translated when it passes through several people. It gets distorted and changed by each person who says the message and who hears the message.

It's proportionally difficult to get a message to all of your staff members. The larger the team, the less likely it will be to see all of them during the week, to pass on the message. Without calling a staff meeting, you will have to rely on others to do it for you. When you want to create that perfection, you can't leave it to chance.

So, how to you rely on others to successfully share your message?

First, you have to make sure your message bearers can deliver the message appropriately. The more important the message, the more important it is to make sure that each person fully understands it. Practice the delivery with them, several times if you need to.

Second, having a paper copy of your message is also good for your employees, so they can refer to it. It's a good way to outline the key points. It can be done as a poster, or as a separate sheet for each person. Just make sure the hard copy isn't the only way your message is delivered. You can be guaranteed there will be some people who won't read it at all, and others that won't really understand what is written, depending on the message. It's better to cover your bases by delivering both a verbal and visual message.

Finally, I suggest making a full list of your employees, and assign each one to a message bearer, including yourself. After each person receives the message, have the bearer put his or her initials by the employee's name. This way you will know that every single person on the team receive the message, and which person delivered the message.

Remember, you should always take the time follow up with your team, to make sure they understood the message fully and to let people know you are there for any questions or assistance. Creating the ultimate experience of the Big Show takes a lot of work, continuous follow up, and attention to detail.

Interpretation

Life is ten percent what happens to you and ninety percent how you respond to it. ~ Lou Holtz

Events are simply events. The way we interpret the events in our lives is what actually gives those events meaning. In fact, it was actually one of my children who helped me understand the real truth in that.

We were at the dinner table one evening, when my daughter lifted up her fork, showing all of us the bent tine. She beamed a smile at everyone and exclaimed, "I got the lucky fork!" The fork still resides in the cutlery drawer; and anytime one of us gets the bent fork, we see it as a great thing.

Far too many of us, myself included at that time, would have thought it unlucky to get a partially dysfunctional fork, and would have either fixed it or thrown it away, missing out on the opportunity to experience something greater from it. It really is all in the interpretation. So, next time you find yourself stuck in traffic, see it as a good thing simply because it gives you more time to enjoy the music on the radio. Perhaps tripping on the sidewalk could be a good message, telling us we need to become more grounded. Who knows? What you come up with will depend on you, and how you choose to interpret it.

Get it?

Perception is reality. Remember it is not what you say or how you say it, but rather what is heard that is important. ~ Ian Gray

Follow up on your communications with your team, to make sure the message was received as you intended to deliver it. Many times, we assume that they get it just as we meant it. Well…you know what happens when you assume, don't you?

No Clones, Please

Take a look at the people who walk into your store. Every one of them is different. They come from different ethnic backgrounds, are different ages, sexes, and so on. Your team needs to reflect that as well.

Many times when looking for sales people, we look for certain traits, like being outgoing and friendly, that dynamic person who can hold the centre of attention. And that will work for some of your customers.

Now think about a very timid and shy person. How comfortable are they with the person who is the life of the party? They aren't. They will probably become more quiet and introverted, because they're uncomfortable around that kind of boisterousness. In a sales situation, these two people aren't going to connect, and that's going to lead to an unsatisfied customer, if they become a customer at all.

Your sales team needs to be as diverse as your clientele. Bring on people who are introverts, as well as extroverts. Have different ethnic backgrounds, different ages, different hair colours, and so on. As long as all of the people you hire are willing to learn how to be great at what they do, you can teach them what they need to know to excel in your store.

The more variety and diversity you have, the more likely you will be able to connect with the majority of your customers, and that leads to better success.

The Last Line of Defence

Leadership does not always wear the harness of compromise. ~ Woodrow Wilson

A customer who was new to my store was dealing with a new salesperson that didn't really know a lot about the products the customer was buying. That was okay with the customer, because the salesperson found someone to help, who had the knowledge the customer needed. She also gave the new salesperson bonus points because he stayed to learn. He helped her as best as he could, and she recognized that. So far, so good. But then, the whole situation moved into a major crisis when she went to check out. The cashier was rude and snippy when she asked a question about pricing, since the price at the register was more expensive than the price listed in the aisle. After begrudgingly fixing the issue, the cashier threw her change down on the counter, and didn't bother to thank her for her purchase, or say goodbye.

Unfortunately, I was able to observe the very end of the transaction, but wasn't able to get to the customer before she walked out. I had no doubt I would receive a complaint letter, and that it would probably take a miracle to get her to shop in the store again. I was right; and to my knowledge, the customer never did come back, although I tried very hard to make it up to her.

I was, however, able to deal with the cashier. I pulled her immediately into the office, where she broke down in tears, and told me her boyfriend had broken up with her, and she was having a very bad day. I made her day worse by terminating her on the spot (she was still under probation).

A hard-nosed line, perhaps. But the bottom line is that she had a choice to come to work that day, or to call in sick. She chose to come to work. She had a choice then to have a good day or a bad day. She made the wrong choice. Worse, she went out of her way to make a customer have a bad day too, and that just can't happen. My job depended on it.

Make no mistake; the behaviour of your employees is a direct reflection of what you allow them to do, and of you as a leader.

Your cashiers are the final impression that leaves with the customer. They are your last line of defence, and one of the most integral parts of your team in creating a lasting experience. So you'd better have cashiers that can make you, rather than break you.

Are You Making Magic?

The great leaders are like the best conductors – they reach beyond the notes to reach the magic in the players. ~ Blaine Lee

How are you going to bring out the magic in each of your team members today?

General Orientation

When it comes to creating the perfection of the Big Show, the details are important. Especially, when it comes to brand new team members. Sometimes, it's the smallest things can make a new person on your team feel much more comfortable. A welcoming smile would be the first. After that, it's nice to know where the bathroom is, the staffroom, first aid kit, emergency exit, and so on.

To get your new team members off to a good start, make sure you have a general orientation plan in place. If you cannot meet them in person, make sure one of your team leaders is there to welcome them to the team and show them around.

A Two-Minute Meeting

Excellent communication is key to great leadership, and the experience of the Big Show. The best way to do that is in person. Whether it's you or another member of your leadership team, you should take a couple of minutes at the beginning of the shift, to review with each team member what they need to know to be successful for the day. That can include sales goals, section assignments or areas of responsibility, new products they need to know about, break times, and so on.

The meeting should always include encouragement and motivation to get them pumped up to start their day, so they can shine in the spotlight.

Two minutes of communication = One Great Day.

Go team!

A Team Building Idea

When you have employees that work in different sections of your store, try creating a game where you pair the employees together to achieve a goal. It's great for team building and camaraderie.

If You're Happy and You Know it, You Can Stay!

Happiness depends upon ourselves. ~ Aristotle

If you have a staff member that is truly having a bad day, the best thing you can do is send them home. The energy of just one person can be highly contagious. Better to have it a happy contagion than a sad one.

One Student, One Trainer

It's always good to remember that people learn differently and at different rates. That's typically why people don't do as well in a group, as they do with one-on-one training.

One-on-one training is less distracting and much more focused on the needs of the individual. It enables the trainer to really judge how well the person is learning the material, while giving them the opportunity to adjust the style and pacing of the training when necessary. The trainer can also adapt to the person's learning style (i.e. visual, auditory, or kinaesthetic), to make it truly effective and long lasting.

People are also more likely to ask questions when they're alone with the trainer. In a group, there is a fear that the question might be viewed as stupid or a waste of time, and so it goes unasked.

Wherever you possibly can, opt for one-on-one training.

The Whole Truth and Nothing But?

One of my favourite and most requested stories to tell while I was training involved a story about a kid we'll call "Dale." I'm pretty sure I've never worked with a Dale, so the identity is safe. And if you are a Dale, and it sounds like you, it's really not about you.

Typically, I act this out to get the full affect, so I hope the translation into the written word is just as amusing for you.

I went in to co-manage a store and assist another manager who was having some difficulty meeting sales goals. One of my first jobs was to evaluate the staff, to make sure the team was effective. I spent my first day just observing the sales on the floor. Dale immediately came to my attention because, for the first 15 minutes of my shift, he followed the other manager around, asking if he could go home.

"Please. I'm so tiii-red," he would whine, making tired a two-syllable word. And he would tug on the manager's shirtsleeve, whining like a three-year-old. "Puuhlease!!"

With an eye roll, the manager would send him off and tell him to go sell something. Within the next hour, Dale was back at the manager's side, again begging to go home.

Yet at another time during the same day, Dale followed behind a customer, slouched over, head lolling on his shoulders, shuffling his feet with the enthusiasm of a teenage girl sporting Uggs. He was dragging a large bag of dog food behind him by one corner, sighing with great hardship as he passed by saying, "I don't want to carry the dog food. It's too heavy. I don't want to carry the dog food."

That was about it for me. I turned to the manager and said, "That kid is a complete pylon and he has to go."

The manager just shook his head, and said, "Let's go check the sales."

Dale consistently had the highest sales in the store every hour he worked. In fact, he greatly surpassed the next best sales person's numbers. How he managed it was completely beyond me, since he seemed to lack any kind of ability; but the numbers clearly showed he was somehow very effective on the floor with the customers.

Dale clearly had a lot of points that needed real coaching (which were worked upon), but that's not really the story here. Sometimes perception and reality of a situation are two very different things. Make sure you have all the facts, before you bring down the judgement.

You've Got Personality

Leaders grow leaders. Developing isn't fixing. ~ Dan Rockwell

There are lots of personality tests out there that you can take, or give to your team, that will give you some insight into the way they work, how they need to receive information, and the best ways you can interact with them. I'm sure every single one of them will be helpful to you as a leader.

One that was presented to me in a seminar by Kevin Graff from The Graff Retail Group was the A.P.L.E Personality Profile. I like it because it's fairly easy and straightforward to complete, which makes it perfect for a 60-minute staff meeting.

The categories break down into Assertive, Passionate, Logical and Easy Going.

People who have Assertive as their dominant personality traits are determined, straightforward and competitive. You would describe them as commanding, confident, bold, and dominant.

Passionate personalities like to focus on other people, and, not surprisingly, are very social. They are usually talkative, bubbly, and like social recognition. They might be described as inspiring, outgoing, and sympathetic.

The Logical person has a need for caution, order and accuracy. They are often task-oriented, and like to focus on his or her standard of proper action. This personality is often described as careful, sensible, accurate, and dependable.

People who fall into the Easy Going style are steady, passive, and people-oriented. They like listening and doing things, but tend to dislike change as it challenges the stability they crave. This person would be described as stable, consistent, friendly, and good-natured.

What I loved most about Kevin Graff's presentation was the way he described the personalities in a grocery store line-up. An Assertive standing in the line would be wondering why they haven't called someone to open up another cash line, as they've noticed that there are no less than three people standing around, who could easily take over a register to get the lines moving. The Passionate personality would be chatting with the cashier, telling her not to worry, it's not her fault, and everything would be okay. The Logical would be counting the items in other people's baskets, to make sure they had less than the 8 items they were supposed to have, in order to stand in the line-up in the first place. And the Easy Going people would just be waiting patiently, because there isn't really anything that can be done about it anyway.

Having an understanding of any person's basic needs, when it comes to their personality style, allows you to adjust your own personality style to suit theirs. For people who are Assertive, you want to give them quick bites of information, and not be too chatty about it. They want to get in, get the job done, and get out. For the Passionate, you should talk with them about their family and personal life a little first, and then talk about what you need them to do, since they have a need to be social, and to connect with you first, before moving into work mode. Logical people will need a lot of information. The more statistics you can give them, the better. They will need hard data to show how this will help, who has done it before, and why it worked in the past. Then they will probably need a little time to digest the information, and make a plan of action before they get started. For the Easy Going people on your team, they are quite happy to complete a task; but if it means change in their life, it will rock their steady foundations, and they won't like it. In this case, you will need to show them how this change will give them greater stability in the future. They need to know it's going to be okay before they get going on it.

No matter what personality test you use, you'll learn more about the people you lead. When you put this information to use, you'll be better able to connect and communicate with them; and when you connect with them in a way they appreciate, they'll be more likely to follow your lead.

Your Physical Store

Be smart about how to set your store up and your business is sure to meet great success.

The Staff Room

The staff room should be a place where everyone on your team can go to rest, relax, and get themselves prepared to bring their best to your customers.

Take a good look at your staff room and ask yourself if it is relaxing or rejuvenating. If not, here are a few things that might help you to transform it into a place your staff will want to go.

1. Clean it up. Most people enjoy a clean and tidy area.
2. Brighten it up. Bright colours can uplift your mood. If you can't paint, try some bright accessories, like pictures or posters on the walls, or colourful throw pillows for a couch or chairs.
3. Make it positive. Make sure the only notes left in the room are ones of congratulations or support. This is not the place to post policy, discipline notes, and so on.
4. Inspire. Post uplifting quotes on a chalkboard or around the room.
5. Kudos. Create colourful and noticeable sheets for staff members to celebrate each other's teamwork, and allow them to post them somewhere in the room. You could also create your own board where you recognize people for their great sales, support, and customer service.

Of course, if you aren't sure what your team might like, getting their input and help will make the task much easier.

Customer Flow

One of the best things you can do for your business is to monitor the number of customers coming through your doors. There are many door counters or people counters on the market that you can choose from, some more high-tech than others; but even a very basic counter will give you a tremendous amount of information that you can use to make your business better.

Firstly, and most obviously, it tells you how many people are walking through your doors each day. This is important to know as it tells you a lot about your traffic patterns throughout the week. It will show you which days have the most and least customers. To get even more in-depth into your customer flow, you can record the flow on an hourly basis, or by particular time blocks during the day. This will allow you to accurately track your busiest periods each day. Analyzing this hard statistical data can allow you to schedule your staff more effectively, by putting more staff on the floor during your busiest days, and at your busiest times during the day. It will help to make your customer service more effective by having the appropriate staffing levels at the right times.

Secondly, using a door counter tells you directly whether or not your marketing initiatives are working. When you know how many people come into your store on any given day, you can measure that against any changes that might happen with the flow when you've placed new advertising, made adjustments to your current marketing plan, or made changes to your window display. If the number of customers that come into your store increases, based on your historical data, then it was a successful endeavour. If the flow doesn't increase, then you need to re-evaluate your marketing decisions.

Next, tracking the number of people coming through your doors allows you to compare that number to the people going through your cash register, giving you your conversion rate. That will help you to track the success of your sales people and your sales managers. For more information on this, read the section on Conversion Rates.

Finally, tracking the customer flow can also alert you to changing factors in your market. A decline in the number of people coming into your store is a definite red flag that can point to a competitor opening in the area, a need for a change in your marketing plan, or worse, it could be a direct reflection of a lack of customer service in your store driving people away. Conversely, an increase could support the fact that you have excellent customer service, and your customers are coming back with their friends.

No matter what way you slice it, tracking your customer flow is a valuable tool that can make your business more successful.

The Physical Experience

Please don't feed the dust bunnies. ~ Author Unknown

Continuous improvement is one of the key factors in the Big Show. Everything counts. Walk through your store with "fresh eyes." What I mean by that is, step outside yourself, and try to look at it the way your customer sees it. When we see the same things day in and day out, we become immune to how they look. We walk past the display that is half filled, and don't really notice that it needs to be replenished. Or we miss the gum or candy wrapper on the floor. We might not even notice when the dust bunnies are reproducing as fast as their beating-heart cousins. But the customer really sees it for what it is, and it makes an impression on them, good or bad.

Start at your front door and evaluate how good your store really looks to your customers.

- What's the first impression they get when they walk in?
- Can a person easily navigate their way through your store?
- What route do they usually take when they walk in?
- How easily can they navigate through your displays?
- What do the displays look like?
- Are the floors clean?
- How is the lighting?
- Is the cashier's area neat and tidy?
- Does the store look dusty?

Doing this kind of walk-through regularly will allow you the opportunity to clean up, make your store look better, and create a better overall customer experience.

Evaluating your traffic flow through the store will tell you a lot about how you can use the store's real estate to its best advantage. For example, placement of your store displays might not allow for a free flow of traffic around your store. They could actually block your customer from entering easily into a particular section. That means a lot of merchandise is getting missed. Moving a display, or adjusting it, might free up the flow of your traffic, and let that merchandise be seen. Or maybe the majority of your customers come into your store and automatically turn right. Then the right-hand side of the entrance is a good place to display your newest products.

From the first impression to the last impression, you want to figure out what your customer sees. Every part of the experience is important. It's a good exercise for you and your management team to do this on a monthly basis. The more eyes, the better as each person will see things from different points of view.

Tidy Up

I have a friend who is a professional organizer. This occupation is rather mindboggling to me. While I'm not extremely messy, being neat like that has been rather a challenge for me most of my life. (My mother and my sister are both vigorously nodding here.) My work area looks like a tornado just came through it most of the time. Let's not even start on my bedroom. My friend, on the other hand, has everything organized, right down to having her makeup sorted and stored by colour, in neatly labelled little pull-out boxes. You can find anything you need in her house or office in seconds, usually by the label. That lets her concentrate on what she needs to do. She's what you would call "streamlined."

My organizational friend gave me some statistics on how much time is wasted looking for those "lost" items. That five minutes you waste looking for your keys each day adds up to 30 hours in a year. She also maintains that the average businessperson spends about an hour a day looking for things he or she knows is on the desk, or in the computer, but can't find easily. That's just over 32 workdays in a year, or 6.5 weeks! It's really an insane waste of time.

That alone is a good reason to clean up the office and your entire store. Imagine how many more customers your staff could help if everything was neat and tidy?

What are You Missing?

You miss 100% of the shots you don't take. ~ Wayne Gretzky

Personally or professionally, do the one thing you've been dreaming about. Who knows where it will take you. One thing is certain, if you never take the first step, you'll never complete the journey.

Break it Down

Management by objectives works if you first think through your objectives. Ninety percent of the time you haven't. ~ Peter Drucker

At the end of a three-day course on management, the leaders in the class had to create a task list of the initiatives they needed to take in their stores, to get moving in the right direction. The list might look like this:

1. Clean up the store
2. Hire new staff members
3. Set up a daily coaching log
4. Set up a coaching schedule
5. Plan a staff meeting

On the surface, this seems like a pretty good plan to get things going. The real issue actually comes when executing the list completely. "Clean up the store" may mean a lot of things to many people. If it's a large format store, it's going to take much more than a day to completely clean the store. Even smaller stores might have difficulty in getting the task done properly in a set amount of time.

The task itself needs to be broken down into smaller steps. On top of that, the leader also has to figure out who is going to oversee each of the steps, how it's going to be completed, which staff members and supervisors will be responsible, and what's the deadline.

Let's break down the steps the leader will actually need to take need to "clean up the store".

1. Break the store into equal sections
2. Assign a leader or supervisor to each section to ensure completion
3. Break down sections into smaller subsections, where necessary, in conjunction with the section supervisor

4. Review assignments with each assigned section supervisor, to ensure a full understanding of the requirements necessary to compete the cleaning
5. Cleaning of the section entails:
   a. Removing all product from the shelves
   b. Washing shelves completely with soapy water
   c. Drying shelves before replacing product
   d. Dusting and/or washing the product
   e. Drying the product
   f. Returning product to shelves, ensuring the label is English side out
   g. Ensuring products are lined up in even rows, flush with the front of the shelf
   h. Checking all products to ensure they are priced properly
   i. Replacing pricing, or pricing products as necessary
   j. Sweeping and mopping under the shelving unit
   k. Sweeping and mopping the floor in the section
6. Review schedule with supervisors, and assign duties to each staff member to assist with the cleaning
7. Assign a deadline for each section, based on the schedule
8. Assign an overall deadline for the project
9. Set follow-up dates before the deadlines, to check progress and assess if help is needed

As you can see, there are many aspects that need to be studied and defined for something as "simple" as cleaning the store completely and effectively by the set deadline. If you have previously been unable to fully complete projects in your store to your satisfaction, this is probably why. Creating the Big Show comes down to the smallest of steps.

Now you know what you need to do to actually "git 'er dun." What initiatives do you need to break down to their individual steps?

Yes Men? No Thank You!

If everyone is thinking alike then somebody isn't thinking. ~ George Patton

Having a team of "yes men" isn't going to challenge you to change the status quo. It's not going to help you create the experience that defines the Big Show. Having someone on your team who doesn't always agree, makes you think. And that means you just might get the opportunity to improve, and start to take the Show to the next level.

See it and Believe it

The only way you can know for sure what's going on in your store is to get out on the floor and see for yourself. The only way you make positive changes is to coach directly on what you see happening. You can't run the Show from behind your desk. So shut off the computer, get out on the sales floor, and show them you got game.

Make Scents

Aromatherapy is a caring, hands-on therapy, which seeks to induce relaxation, to increase energy, to reduce the effects of stress and to restore lost balance to mind, body and soul. ~ Robert Tisserand

We can all use a little help now and then with our mood, mental clarity, or energy. Why not keep a few essential oils on hand in your office to help you out when you need it? Scents like lavender or chamomile can help to relax and de-stress, or citrus scents can help to energize. There are many places you can learn about the benefits of aromatherapy and essential oils, both on-line and in person.

At the very least, you will have a great smelling office.

Goals Obtained

Always aspire, obtain, then start again!

How Do *You* Spell Success?

Success means something different to everyone; or at least, the way we view how we are successful in our lives is different for everyone. Figuring out your personal vision of success, will help you stay focused on the things that are most important and helpful to you.

Webster's Dictionary defines success as "a favourable or desired outcome," like achieving fame or wealth. Yet, I believe that those things come as a by-product of your success. For example, in order for you to become a famous actor or actress, you first have to be successful at acting. The fame and money come after you've focused on fulfilling your goal to be the best actor or actress you can be.

When you really think about it, I bet the times you've felt the most successful were the times when you were truly passionate about what you were doing, when you felt you were doing something that had true meaning for you, and filled you with a sense of purpose. It was a time when everything you were doing fulfilled your true potential. Those are the times that you are truly being the most successful in your life.

Focus on doing more of your successful things and everything else will follow.

Set Goals

In order to continually get better in the Big Show, you need to know what you're working toward. Setting a goal creates a tangible target, which keeps you moving forward to achieve greater success. If there is no goal, there is nothing to reach for, and nothing to achieve. That's why creating goals for you and your team members are necessary for success.

Often as leaders, we set goals for the people on our team who are struggling. They need help, so we coach them and show them the steps they need to take in order to improve their skills; and then we give them a specific goal to hit. For example, if someone is struggling with their average sale statistics, we might train and coach on how to select the proper features and benefits of a product to create real value for the customer. We might then set a goal for them to increase their average sale by $1.00 before the next meeting, using this new knowledge. Setting the goal to increase their average sale by $1.00 defines exactly what they need to do achieve success.

You also need to remember to set goals for your most successful team members. These people often get forgotten simply because they do their jobs so well. Those are the people you want to keep engaged and reaching for greater success, because they are so good at what they do. You want to make sure you don't lose them because they don't feel challenged, or expendable, anymore.

Set goals for each person on your team, including yourself. Write them down (in pen), because once it's written, it's permanent. When you and your team reach your goals, it's celebration time! You've achieved a great thing, and as a leader, isn't that your goal?

The 80/20 Rule

Pareto's Principle states that 20% of something is always responsible for 80% of the results. For you, in retail terms, that means:

- 20% of your customers contribute to 80% of your sales
- 20% of your sales people produce 80% of your sales
- 20% your products make up 80% of your sales

Conversely:

- 80% of your time is spent on 20% of your people
- 80% of your profits come from 20% of the work you do each day
- 80% of your efforts contribute to 20% of your best results

It makes you pause and think, what if you spent more time doing the 20% of things that make you and your team more effective? That would definitely be a better use of time overall. If you know that 20% of your sales people are contributing to 80% of your sales, doesn't it makes sense to put 80% of your time into coaching and supporting that 20%? Instead, we usually do the opposite. We put 80% of our time into focusing on the 20% of the people that are never going to be effective for us anyway. Rather shocking, when it's put in no uncertain terms, isn't it?

So, in order to be a truly effective leader, reset your focus on the things and people you know are working for you. Start supporting the 20% of your staff that are your superstars. Get to know the 20% of the customers that come into your store regularly, and do something special for them, to make sure they keep coming back. And figure out which 20% of your workload is the most effective way for you to spend your time.

Goal Break Down

Setting goals is the first step in turning the invisible into the visible. ~ Tony Robbins

Like any large task, breaking down your monthly sales goal into smaller goals will help you and your team strive to achieve more realistic numbers. Large numbers can be daunting, but when you take that big number and break it down to a number that's easier to comprehend, it will be easier to attain. In order to do that, you need to be able to break down your monthly goal into a daily goal. But calculating that goal is more complex than just dividing the monthly sales goal by the number of days in the month. Statistically speaking, you don't sell the same amount of goods on Wednesday than you do on Saturday. Saturday is typically the busiest day of the week for retailers, so you can expect to do more sales on a Saturday than you would on a Wednesday. Breaking down your monthly goal needs to reflect those sales differences, in order for you to have a good measurement of the sales you need to achieve on any given day.

Sales are predictable. While you might not be able to predict the exact amount of sales you will do on any given Monday, you can look at your past sales to predict an estimate of what you can expect to do on any given Monday. You do that by looking at your historical data to get your sales averages for each day of the week. This data needs to be analyzed over a period of a few weeks to get an appropriate average.

Let's say you take four weeks of sales data, ensuring you have an equal amount of Mondays, Tuesdays, Wednesdays, etc. Add together the sales totals of all the Mondays, and divide by the number of Mondays, which in this case will be four, to get the average amount of sales you do on a Monday. For example:

Monday #1 = $2230.00
Monday #2 = $2050.60
Monday #3 = $2130.40
Monday #4 = $2191.00

The complete sales total for the Mondays are $8602.00. Divide that by four Mondays to get the average Monday sales.

$8602.00/4 = $2150.50

Complete the averages for each day of the week. Once you have the average days done, you add the average days together, to get an average week of sales.

Your complete break down for average daily sales might look like this:

Monday = $2150.50
Tuesday = $2150.50
Wednesday = $1720.40
Thursday = $2580.60
Friday = $3225.75
Saturday = $5376.25
Sunday = $4301.00

That means, in your average week, you can expect to do about $21 505.00 in sales, based on the sum of the daily averages.

From there, you need to break down the percentage of sales you will do on a Monday, Tuesday, Wednesday, and so on, so you can apply this data to your currently monthly goal.

In order to get your daily sales percentage, you divide the average daily sales by the average weekly sales, and multiply it by 100. Let's calculate the percentage of sales we can expect to do on a Monday, based on the numbers previously generated.

($2150.50/$21 505.00) X 100 = 10%

After completing the calculations based on numbers noted above, you will find that your daily sales percentages break down like this:

Monday: 10%
Tuesday: 10%
Wednesday: 8%

Thursday: 12%
Friday: 15%
Saturday: 25%
Sunday: 20%

Now, let's say you've been set a monthly goal of $100 000, and the month has 30 days. We now need to break that down into a weekly amount, so we can apply the daily sales percentages we just calculated, to get the goal we need to reach for each day of the week.

$100 000/30 days = $3333.33 per day average

$3333.33 X 7 days = $23 333.31

That means in a week your goal will be $23 333.31

Once you have your 7-day goal, you use your daily sales averages to get a more accurate goal for each day of the week. Now, you will multiply the weekly goal by the daily percentages.

Monday: $23 333.31 X 10% = $2333.33
Tuesday: $23 333.31 X 10% = $2333.33
Wednesday: $23 333.31 X 8% = $1866.67
Thursday: $23 333.31 X 12% = $2800.00
Friday: $23 333.31 X 15% = $3500.00
Saturday: $23 333.31 X 25% = $5833.32
Sunday: $23 333.31 X 20% = $4666.66

The numbers we just generated are more accurate and achievable goals to set for each day. One thing you do have to remember is to add any shortfalls you may have into your goals for the rest of the week. For example, if you missed Monday's goal by $100, then Tuesday's goal must change to become $2433.33. If you beat the goal for the day, I would suggest leaving the goal at the currently planned target. Why lower expectations? You want to continue to grow your sales. Adjusting the target to a lower number will only have you reaching the bar, rather than leaping over it.

Daily goals can be broken down even further so you can see if you're achieving the numbers set for you, throughout the day. Again, you probably don't sell as much in the morning as you do later in the day. In the same way you broke down the numbers to get your average Monday, Tuesday, Wednesday, etc., you can also do the same thing to get the average sales you can expect to do in the morning, afternoon and evening.

For example, Monday might break down like this:

Morning (10am-1pm) = 20%
Afternoon (2pm-5pm) = 30%
Evening (6pm-9pm) = 50%

Based on our goal of $2150.50 for the day, that would mean our sales goals for each period during the day on Monday would look like this:

Morning – $2150.50 X 20% = $430.10
Afternoon – $2150.50 X 30% = $645.15
Evening – $2150.50 X 50% = $1075.25

The nice thing about knowing exactly where you're supposed to be for sales at any point during the day is that it allows you to do something about it right away if you aren't reaching those goals. For example, if I checked my sales on Monday at 6pm, I should have an accumulation of $1075.25 in sales if I'm on track to meet my goal for the day. (Add the morning and afternoon goals together to get $1075.25.) If I'm over the goal, I can give everyone a high five. If I'm under the goal, I need to do something about it, like play a game to focus on add-on sales, adjust coaching and directing styles on the sales floor, focus more on sales and less on operations, whatever it takes to get the sales up to where they're supposed to be.

By breaking down the goals and tracking your sales against those goals, you have the ability to be proactive. You can't do anything about the past, but you sure have the ability to change the future.

Final Words

Your ability to touch this world does not start at your shoulder and end with your fingertips. It comes from the strength and determination inside you.

Thank you for reading. I hope you've found a few things to help you on your way to being the best leader you can be and creating your very own version of the Big Show.

~Andrea

References

Albom, Mitch. *Tuesdays with Morrie*. New York: Doubleday, 1997.

Graff Retail. www.graffretail.com. Piggybank Technology. n.d.

Lundin, Stephen C., et. al. *Fish! A Remarkable Way to Boost Morale and Improve Results*. New York: Hyperion, 2009.

Orwell, George. *Animal Farm*. New York: Penguin Group Incorporated, 1996.

Seuss, Dr. *Oh the Places You'll Go*. New York: Beginner Books, Random House, 1986.

Sharma, Robin. *Who will Cry for You When You Die?* New York: HarperCollins Publishers Ltd., 1999.

Sinek, Simon. *Start with WHY: How Great Leaders Inspire Everyone to Take Action*. New York: Penguin Books , 2011.

Williams, Roy H. *Secret Formulas of the Wizard of Ads: Turning Paupers into Princes and Lead into Gold*. Austin: Bard Press 1999

www.ingramcontent.com/pod-product-compliance
Lightning Source LLC
Chambersburg PA
CBHW051905170526
45168CB00001B/247